YOU

ARE

NEVER

ALONE

Osayi Ogieva

God bless you!

YOU
ARE
NEVER
ALONE

BE CONFIDENT IN
THE PROMISE OF
GOD'S PRESENCE

Osayi Ogieva

XULON PRESS

Xulon Press
2301 Lucien Way #415
Maitland, FL 32751
407.339.4217
www.xulonpress.com

Printed in the United States of America.

ISBN-13: 9781545613030

TABLE OF CONTENTS

ACKNOWLEDGEMENTS

IT TOOK A dedicated and loving village to have this book delivered from my heart to your hands.

To my loving husband, Dr. Levi Oke-Ifidon, I say thank you for your patience, love, prayers, and understanding. Your support and encouragement kept me going and gave me the strength to finish writing this book.

I am grateful to God for my Pastor, Daniel Adewumi and his wife, Grace Daniels for their constant prayers, counsel, and encouragement. I will never forget your kindness towards me. Your love for God and people has greatly inspired me.

I say big thanks to Pastor Tope Akinsiku, who devotedly read my manuscript through the lens of a spiritual authority and provided insightful feedback for its improvement. Five years ago, you gave me the opportunity to be a contributor for your ministry's magazine and that was the first time I had written anything in that context. I discovered my writing gift as I embraced the opportunity. Thank you for seeing in me what I did not see in myself at that time.

May the Lord bless and reward Paul Ekhaesomi Jnr., a professional editor who edited the first draft of this book without collecting a cent from me. Thank you for all the inspirational messages you sent me and shared with me. I am honored to call you my friend. You have the kindest heart ever.

To Chinyelu Onuorah and Gladys Ebireri, I am grateful for your availability to read my manuscripts anytime of the day. Thank you for the suggestions on how to protect the identities in this book.

A big thanks to Dawn and Terry Magee, of Rising Oaks Ministries for all their love, encouragement, and prayers.

To Deaconness Lanre Mebude, Deacon Paul Ugobor, Ehi Ade-Mabo, Esosa Agbonifo, and Aike Naomi, thank you for believing in me, and in this message. I appreciate all the words of encouragement, advise and prayers. There was not a month that went by without one of you asking if my book was complete. Thank you for that subtle push.

I am grateful to Kerri-Ann of Conclusio House Publishing for the final professional editing. You did a great job.

May God bless Pastor Daniel Adewumi, Pastor Wale Akinsiku, and Pastor Bayo Adediran for their spiritual investments in me. Your teachings have impacted my life in many positive ways.

Importantly, I will like to thank God for giving me a personal encounter with Him. Never again will I doubt your presence in my life, or your love for me. Thank you for making impossibilities, possible in my life. Thank you for inspiring me to write. You guided me so personally and I know that I accomplished this because You were with me.

DEDICATION

I dedicate this book to my lovely family:

My dear father, Mr. Daniel Nosa Ogieva who passed away before I completed writing this book. Until his death, he was my biggest cheerleader and supporter. My daughter-father experience with him made it easy for me to understand and embrace God's love for me. You believed in me so much and never held back in giving me all I needed to grow and be successful in life. Thank you for everything you did for me and for believing in me when no one else did. I miss you every day. May you continue to find rest in the Lord's bosom in Jesus name, Amen.

To my amazing mother, Gladys Ogieva, who by example has taught me hospitality, kindness, and generosity. You motivate me to be the best version of myself. Thank you for being a pillar of strength and support to me. I love you so much.

My life will be less exciting without my three siblings – Isoken, Amena, and Idahosa. I could never imagine life without you guys. Your overwhelming support and love for me has kept me standing in good and challenging times. I love you and I pray that you experience the resurrection power of Jesus Christ in your individual lives. Amen.

INTRODUCTION

DRY. BARREN. NO one in sight to wipe away her tears. None to warmly embrace her and speak soothing words to heal her broken heart. Her feet had become callused by wandering. Her body worn out by thirst and starvation. Circumstances had placed her in the wilderness—a place devoid of hope, characterized by bleakness and discomfort.

Having walked a while, she found a spring in the desert. It was too good to be true. An oasis, right in the midst of dryness. Quickly, she satisfied her thirst and sat down, giving herself time to rest and ponder her present situation. She was alone.

In the silence of her environment, it was evident that no one was looking for her. She would have heard her name being called out by her boss, from whom she had run away. It didn't matter what her mistakes were, no one deserves to be so uncared for, unwanted, unloved, and unsupported.

She was Hagar, Sarai's maid. There were many promises God made to Abram, Sarai's husband. These were the promises of abundance, greatness, influence, dignity, and wealth. Years after, Abram was on the right path of God's plan for him and began to see these spoken vows become his reality. In Genesis 15:1, we see God make another promise to him, *"Do not be afraid, Abram, I am your shield; Your reward [for obedience] shall be very great."*

Despite the blessings of God in Abram's life, he still desired to have a child. Upon hearing the vow God just made to him, Abram replied saying, *"Lord God, what reward will You give me, since I am [leaving this world] childless, and he who will be the owner and heir of my house is this [servant] Eliezer from Damascus?"* And Abram continued, *"Since You have given no child to me, one (a servant) born in my house is my heir"* (Genesis 15:2-3, AMP). Nothing else mattered to Abram if he had no child! Not the wealth. Or the abundance. Or the influence. This turned out to be a defining moment as God promised him a child that will come from "his own body" (Genesis 15:4).

It was this promise from God to Abram that began Hagar's journey into the intimate details of the woman she served as a maid. As Abram and his wife, Sarai were past child-bearing age, Sarai assumed that the God that prospered, protected, and provided for them could not bring the child through her. She suggested that her husband have sexual relations with her maid to "assist God" in bringing to pass what He had promised. Hagar's pregnancy turned out to be a blessing and a burden at the same time to Sarai as Hagar began disrespecting, and resenting her. When Sarai retaliated, Hagar ran into the desert for her safety. There are times we find ourselves in the desert as a direct consequence of our actions. Sometimes, we end up here due to our inactions, the acts of others, or circumstances beyond our control.

Have you ever stepped into the shoes of this woman called Hagar? Worse, have you ever walked in them? Your emotions run deep, and there are no arms to comfort you. The bills keep piling up, your credit cards are all maxed out, and you still have no income source. Maybe you are in a new environment and feel unaccepted and unwelcome. Or maybe the medical test results came in, and the doctor needs to see you urgently. Trials have a way of making us feel alone, but in the midst of it all stands someone who is interested in us and the circumstances that have befallen us. God knew, before we ever did, that we would sometimes arrive in the wilderness. Regardless of the journey that leads us to this place, God makes it all work together for our good. He places streams in the desert as an expression of His love for us—the spot-on word of encouragement to keep us going; the provision to meet our needs; the friend who knows someone who knows someone else to help us get that interview; the healing testimonies of others who overcame a similar health challenge to build our faith muscles.

We, like Hagar, who is the character in this story, get so consumed by the presence of the "stream"—His presents to us—that we forget that it is only indicative of something more significant—God's presence. In Hebrews 13:5b, God says, *"I will never desert you, nor will I ever forsake you"* (NASB). And when we pay attention, really close attention, we will realize that He is indeed closer than we think. Hagar did. Not by choice, but through the quietness that enveloped her environment. .

God's presence guarantees His presents.

"Hagar," she heard her name being called. She had been by herself since her journey began. Who else was there with her?

"And He said, 'Hagar, Sarai's maid, where did you come from and where are you going?' And she said, 'I am running away from my mistress Sarai'" (Genesis 16:8 AMP).

In a place of aloneness, confusion, and despair, in a place where she least expected to be discovered, she was found. Not by any mortal, but by God, who desired to turn an uneventful season into a lifetime encounter. God affirmed her, a person considered unimportant in the eyes of others, with the gift of His presence.

Though the Scriptures state that an angel met Hagar, we need to remember that messengers are as significant as the person they represent. The Bible is full of people who rejoiced at angelic visitations, because it meant that

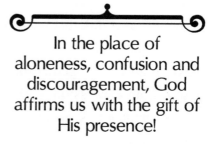

In the place of aloneness, confusion and discouragement, God affirms us with the gift of His presence!

God saw them, was with them, and knew where they were. Mary was one such person (Luke 1:28-30). Mary's life transformed after her encounter with the angel, and so did Hagar's.

The stream supplied Hagar's needs temporarily, but recognizing God's presence brought her guidance, a solution, and hope for the future (Genesis 16:9-11). Genesis 16 shows us that God hears every word we speak in the wilderness. He sees every tear that falls and, amazingly, He responds. It is one thing to know about God, it is entirely another thing to know Him. What an encounter Hagar had!

We are never alone. The wilderness experience can make us resent the only One who can turn things around. However, we need to remember that no circumstance can swallow us beyond God's reach (Isaiah 59:1). It is His presence, not His presents that sustains us as we go through harsh experiences (Isaiah 43:1-2). It is

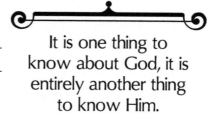

It is one thing to know about God, it is entirely another thing to know Him.

His presence that leads us out triumphantly (Isaiah 43:19). Only

when we listen and watch out for this presence can we exclaim, like Hagar did, *"Have I not even here [in the wilderness] remained alive after seeing Him [who sees me with understanding and compassion]?"* (Genesis 16:13 AMP).

If you are going through a wilderness experience in any area of your life, or feel alone in your circumstance, be assured of one thing—you are not alone. God is in it with you. And if you search expectantly for Him, you will find Him, right next to you, just like I did.

The night season of my life felt so long. Never have I felt so emotionally and physically alone. But the voice that spoke to me, the hands that held me up, the love I could not reject, and the comfort that eased my pain were all markers of His presence. God gave me the most transformative experience of my Christian life yet. He revealed Himself to me as One who longs to be personal and intimate with me.

Journey with me as I share stories of my encounter with the Holy Spirit—God's Spirit. While my journey may be different from yours, this book will help you to understand who the Holy Spirit is, and why He is a relevant part of our lives. In this book, you will also learn how the Holy Spirit speaks, how to develop intimacy with Him, and what can hinder our communication and relationship with Him. Finally, you will learn to recognize His voice in the midst of other voices.

I pray this book blesses you with a deeper understanding of the Holy Spirit and makes you thirst for more of His presence, as you do His presents, in your life.

Chapter One

SOMETHING'S MISSING

"Now the donkeys belonging to Saul's father Kish were lost, and Kish said to his son Saul, 'Take one of the servants with you and go and look for the donkeys'" (1 Samuel 9:3 NIV).

OPENING OUR EYES and seeing the dawn of a new day is enough reason to have hope, knowing we have another shot on this side of eternity. For some, it's a time of gratitude, or a time to set expectations for the day, or a time to pray. However, I would stay awake on my bed, saddened to still find myself in this place of hopelessness and utter discomfort. I was tired of living this way, even though I had no clue how I should be living.

Here I was, unhappy with what many would feel privileged to have—a loving and supportive family, a good career, wonderful friends, and a dynamic church family. The things and places I once enjoyed had suddenly become irritating to me.

"There's got to be more to life than what I am currently living," I constantly thought to myself.

Nothing appealed to me anymore. Do not get me wrong, I dearly loved my family, friends, church, and job, but there was an emptiness within me that these could not fill, no matter how hard I tried. My job suddenly went from being the thing I looked forward to doing daily to being a chore, making every moment there torturous. I knew it was time to leave, so I began my job hunt while holding on tightly to what I still had.

For months, I applied to several organizations in the city where I lived and neighbouring cities as well. My résumé must have been lost in a pile at these agencies, since I never received a rejection letter. Rejection letters, though painful to accept, help me know my application was received and my efforts appreciated. I prayed, fasted, sowed financial seeds, but nothing seemed to work. Frustrated, I bared all my concerns to my friend, Lara. I desperately needed to vent. Was there a DNH (Do Not Hire) database somewhere with my name on it? I wouldn't know. I thought they said it is easier to find a job when you are currently employed. My case was obviously different.

"You should try looking for a job elsewhere," she said. "There are lots of opportunities here in Saskatchewan."

I believed her. Her career had skyrocketed since she made her move there a year ago. It did not take too long to convince me. I desperately needed a new job, and if making a complete change of environment would help me to achieve that, I did not mind. So, my second phase of job hunting began.

It was not easier or automatic on this side as I'd hoped, but Lara, confident that I would pull through in no time, urged me on. Also joining my cheering bandwagon was Harry.

Harry and I met months after my second job hunting phase began. Soon after, we started a relationship, and his presence in my life heightened my desire for open career doors in Saskatchewan. I certainly did not want a long distance relationship, but I also did not want to be bankrupt in my quest to be loved.

In no time, the doors flung open. Within two weeks, I received phone calls for three different interviews from reputable organizations. I became excited because of this prospect. An interview was worth celebrating, considering how long I had searched with no feedback from any organization. My file was now finally off the shelf. Weeks later, I accepted a job offer.

The lines were suddenly falling into pleasant places for me (Psalm 16:6). I was over the moon about this new opportunity. It represented a new career path, increased benefits, greater financial compensation, and a promising relationship. Despite my excitement, when the time came for me to get the ball rolling, I became nervous. Although I was going to be in Saskatchewan, my work location was hours away from everyone else I knew.

Saskatchewan has two major cities—Regina, its capital, and Saskatoon. Lara, Harry, and everyone else I knew in Saskatchewan lived in Saskatoon. My new offer was in neither cities, but towns and hours away from both. Suddenly, it became apparent that a job relocation was only as appealing to me as the support system I had in place. I am not one of those adventurous people who love to explore new places and new things. I was afraid to step into an unknown territory. I was frightened to go where I knew no one. I was frozen with fear and on the verge of remaining where I was, but the uneasiness and discomfort I felt in my present location would not let me. It took weeks, but I finally did make a move. A slight move. I took an inch of a step of faith—I decided to take a tour before relocation.

The bus arrived at the town a few minutes to midnight. I had earlier flown to Regina and boarded a bus to the town.

"Is...is this the place?" I stood there, asking the driver with confusion written all over my face.

He had recently announced that we were minutes away from our destination. As I gazed through the window, all I could see was thick darkness. I could stretch out my palm and hold some of it.

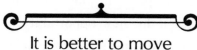

It is better to move forward in faith than remain stagnated by fear.

"You've never been here before?" he asked as he turned aside and stared briefly at me.

"Yes," I whispered.

The town was so quiet that my steps while exiting the bus could be heard miles away.

"You will be okay. Just walk into that convenience store right around the corner and wait for your ride to where you'll be staying." This time he looked at me reassuringly.

A harsh cold wind welcomed me the moment I stepped off the bus. It was winter here already; a shocking difference from the cool weather back home in Vancouver. The trucks driving through the town supplied me with two things I needed at that time—noise and lights. The blaring sounds kept me alert. The bright light rays illuminated my path to the convenience store.

I wondered why the buses only came this way at night. I pulled out the paper on which I had written the phone numbers of local cab drivers and the hotel I'd be lodging. I called a cab. The store turned out to be the perfect landmark for my pick up.

The driver and I chatted as he drove. He was quite inquisitive, wanting to know my intention for moving here. He painted beautiful pictures of the town for me with his words. The rich history, the community's hospitality, the social and cultural attractions, and the harsh winter conditions. For some reason, I did not feel threatened by him.

In the morning, I dashed out for a quick survey of the town. Since I would not be arriving with a car, I decided it would be ideal to test the transit system. However, it was not readily available, as buses did not go through all the routes; a big no-no for me. Other than that, the cab driver was right. The people were warm, friendly, and unsurprisingly curious. The taxi driver did tell

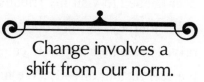
Change involves a shift from our norm.

me to expect that. Shopping options were limited as well. Indeed, it was a one-hundred-and-eighty degree turn from my usual environment. Wasn't this what I thought I wanted? Could this be my answered prayer?

By evening, I could tell that the cab driver was right about the community's hospitality. From my interaction with some of the residents, I could feel the love and warmth in the town. Their smiles, curiosity, receptiveness, willingness to help with directions and answer the questions I had were all welcoming. Many were shocked to hear about my intended leap from a big city to a relatively small town.

Before heading back to Regina, I made accommodation reservations, just in case I became brave enough to take the plunge. From Regina, I boarded the bus heading to Saskatoon to spend the weekend with my friends before returning home. I could not wait to share the details of my trip to this town.

It was almost midnight when the bus arrived in Saskatoon, and I was exhausted from all the travelling. Lara was awaiting me at the depot where we disembarked from the bus. As I shared my experience with her, fear reared its ugly head, again. This time around, I was afraid of being isolated. That day trip made me realize that if I ever needed to visit my friends or boyfriend, it would take half-a-day's journey. Furthermore, to visit my family meant a four-hour drive to Regina's airport to catch a flight. Thinking about this made me feel distant already. We had barely made it inside the house when I let her know I would be giving my job hunt one final try. I quickly brought out my laptop and in a job search that lasted less than ten minutes, I came across an opportunity that caught my attention. The posting was going to be taken down in ninety minutes!

Unlike the job in the town that was going to be a new professional experience, this position shared some similarities with what I was currently doing at work in Vancouver, but distinctively different at the same time. What was better? It was going to be in

Regina. Though exhausted, I began the application process for this opportunity and made it right in time for submission.

———————◆———————

The alarm bells of discomfort and uneasiness went off the moment I returned home in Vancouver, and they got louder as I resumed work on Monday morning. Refusing to fight it any longer, I submitted my resignation letter and courageously accepted the offer in the town. I could not let my indecisiveness steal such an opportunity from me.

People close to me raised their eyebrows about my decision to leave a big city where I had a family, and move to a town where I knew no one. Friends questioned if it had to do with my relationship with Harry. But I had been feeling this way for almost a year, long before he surfaced in my life. His presence in my life, however, encouraged me through it all. His support, as well as Lara's, enabled me to keep going when the application process got overwhelming. Their presence in Saskatchewan gave me hope that I would not be in isolation, though we would be hours apart.

Though my finances were not in shape for my intended relocation, I put together the little money I had and, on a stringent budget, began to prioritize. I set aside just enough money for my rent, food, and transportation. I used the balance to prepare myself for this leap.

———————◆———————

The day I left Vancouver was indeed unforgettable. Never in my life had so many things gone wrong in such a relatively short period of time. My only appointment that day, which was the hair-dresser, went by quickly. In no time I was on my way back home to pick up my luggage and head to the airport. I was minutes away from the hairdresser when I realized that my cell phone was not in my possession. With the journey ahead of me, I could not afford to lose my contacts and means of communication. Returning to pick up my phone, I got off the bus and, unfortunately, had to go in the opposite direction. Luckily, I found my cell on the seat where I left it. To ensure that I arrived home before rush hour, I flagged down a cab and, once inside, asked the driver to go as fast as he could.

Just when I was settling comfortably in the cab, my phone rang. "This isn't the time," I muttered under my breath, carefully removing the items in my purse in search of my phone, again. At least I knew it was in there.

A quick glance at the caller ID revealed an unfamiliar number with Saskatchewan's area code. I quickly answered it.

"Hello, Osayaa," the caller said, as he struggled to accurately say my name. "I hope I pronounced your name right?"

Not wanting to give a speech on how to rightly pronounce my name, I responded affirmatively.

"My name is Michael," the caller continued. "You responded to a job application several weeks ago in Regina, and we would like to schedule an interview with you."

I should have been excited but was, instead, perturbed.

"I am sorry," I said. "I did apply to multiple related jobs in recent times. Could you be more specific on this job application?"

When he specified, it turned out to be the job posting I had responded to the night I returned from the town's exploration.

What a coincidence that they were contacting me just hours before my move there.

"Umm. Sure, I would be available," I said as we agreed to the interview date and time.

I was starting to get frantic at the traffic already building up, and could not hide my apprehension.

"There are alternate routes I can take to get you home soon," the cab driver assured me. I only had three hours to pick up my luggage from my house, bid my family goodbye, and get to the airport.

Mentally, I began calculating what missing my flight would mean for my finances, should that happen. My phone rang again, breaking my thoughts. It was my sister, Mena, calling.

"Osayi, one of your bags just broke," she said. "Please make a quick stop at the mall and buy another, as there is no available one in the house to use."

Argh! I wanted to scream loudly at no one in particular. An appointment at the beauty salon was all I had set out for that day. How did I end up running around in circles? The cab driver had to reroute as we quickly headed to the store.

"Dear Lord, let me make it on time to the airport," I prayed.

I had not planned for these discouraging detours. My thoughts quickly raced from fear of missing my flight to anger at the unnecessary and unforeseen expenses and to doubts. I began questioning my decision to relocate in the first place.

"Were these signs for me to cancel my plans and remain in Vancouver? Or were they hindrances to discourage me from moving forward?" I asked myself.

Not knowing the right answer, I picked up my phone and called Harry. I was frustrated, tired, and confused. He listened to my complaints and remained silent for a while.

"Have you realized that the job interviews you have in Saskatchewan are all in Regina, except the town? It's surprising you got no interviews in Saskatoon, where everyone you know resides," he said.

That was an interesting insight. I knew I had no support system in the town or even in the city closest to it, Regina. But it never dawned on me that of all the interviews I had, none came from Saskatoon, but all from Regina. Except for the town.

Harry could not answer my question. This move was about me. I had to make my decision.

Hurrying out of the store with a new suitcase, I quickly dashed into a new cab to go home and pick up my bags. In retrospect, I could have asked my sister to meet me at the airport with them, but I made it back home sooner than I thought.

Our goodbyes, though genuine, were very quick. I only had two hours to arrive at the airport, go through security, and board the plane. Not enough time, if you ask me.

I hurried to the check-in line. Thankfully, it wasn't a long one. But I would soon find out why.

"I am sorry, check in for that flight is closed. Passengers are already boarding. If you had no luggage, it would have been easier," said the airline's check-in agent. "It is too late to check in your luggage, and you would not make it through security on time. You will have to board the next plane."

I stood facing everything I'd feared. I was exhausted, mentally and physically.

"How many bags have you got?" she asked.

Counting them, I stopped at three.

"Are you aware you will be paying for two additional bags?" she asked.

I nodded in agreement.

"To get on the next flight, you will have to pay the difference," she concluded, calculating on her system how much it was going to be.

Running around Vancouver in a cab was never a part of my plan. Purchasing a bag, no matter how affordable, was a luxury I could not afford. The total of my unplanned expenses was not high but, in comparison to what I had, was significant. What a day. Time, money, energy, all wasted, and still I did not get on the plane.

"What is God trying to say to me in this mess?" I asked myself countless times.

I walked towards an empty seat I saw a few steps from where I was standing, and sank into it. I had three hours till the next flight, so I decided to rest mentally before going through security.

I could hear my phone vibrating. This time around, I was deliberately not answering it. My energy had run out. But whoever the caller was, he or she was dead set on reaching me, as the phone kept ringing.

It was my sister, again. "Osayi, are you boarding now?" she asked.

"No," I responded, letting out a long and profound sigh.

"Great, because you left your carry-on suitcase at home."

I think I wanted to cry. Or laugh. Whatever it was, it appeared I was under God's radar that day. A part of me wanted to cancel every arrangement I'd made, forget this opportunity, and return home to prepare for my upcoming interview in Regina. Another big part of me was ready to move forward, regardless. What a disaster it would be to reject this offer and not get the other one. Still, the third part of me wanted to sleep and forget about everything. I owed myself that.

Hours later, I sat relaxed on the plane headed to Regina with my three bags and my carry-on suitcase. From there, I would board the bus to the town that I would call home.

Chapter Two

GONE WITH THE WIND

"The old has gone, the new is here!" (2 Corinthians 5:17b NIV).

I PREPARED FOR my first day at my new job with much enthusiasm. I invested time in choosing my outfit, shining my shoes, and restyling my hair. Using Google search engine, I pulled up phone numbers of taxi companies and requested one.

The cab driver had an unusual look on his face as he saw me walking towards the car. After exchanging pleasantries, I got comfortable in the seat and handed him the address to my new office. I was elated beyond words for this new beginning. Just me, a new location, no family, no friends. What an adventure for someone so people-oriented. I could not wait to see what life had in store for me here.

Out of the blue, I heard the driver say excitedly, "You came back!"

"Sorry. What? Are you talking to me?" I asked, confused, my eyes focused on the cab meter. Google map had told me it was going to be a ten-minute ride, but this seemed to be taking longer.

Every extra minute mattered, as it meant more money for me. I'd thrown away money running from one end of Vancouver to another.

"Yes," he replied. "You don't remember me? A month ago you visited this town, and I was the driver that picked you up from the convenience store to the lodge where you spent the night. I remember you."

It was both incredible and creepy at the same. The driver recounted his experience with me and was surprised I decided to return.

"How long do you plan on staying here?" he asked rhetorically. "From a city as big as Vancouver to this town. It's going to be a big change for you. A big change," he added.

As we arrived at my destination, I thanked him and paid him for the ride.

He turned his face, smiled, and instead of receiving the money, handed me his business card. "Call me when your work day is almost over. I will come get you. Enjoy your first day at work."

Huh? I tried persuading him to accept payment, but he adamantly declined.

"God, I am no longer under the radar. You see me," I thought, with a big smile on my face. The Bible assures us in Psalm 139 that we are never lost beyond God's reach. He is wherever we are.

"Where can I go from your Spirit? Where can I flee from your presence? If I go up to the heavens, you are there; if I make my bed in the depths, you are there" (Psalm 139:7-8 NIV).

God supplied my need according to His resources, as the Scriptures tell us in Philippians 4:19. He knew I did not have much left after my merry-go-round in Vancouver. "Indeed, Lord, you now see me." I could not deny that this was God at work.

Minutes before I clocked out, I called the cab driver, and he arrived right on schedule to take me home. This time, he offered me a deal. He would drive me anywhere within the town at a fifty percent discounted rate. It felt like a dream, a good one.

Gradually, I began settling in, making peace with my new environment. Many evenings were physically lonely, and sometimes I took myself for a walk on those cold nights. But my siblings, friends and Harry were available to chat with over the phone.

Two weeks later, I met a lady called Adanma. Like me, she had her roots in Nigeria, but had since found a home in this lovely small town in Saskatchewan, where she lived with her husband and two daughters. An elderly gentleman who met me in the coffee shop became the bridge that linked us.

"Where are you from?" the elderly man had asked me, stylishly tucking the question into a conversation we were having about the weather.

"Vancouver," I said, then quickly added, "but I was born and raised in Nigeria."

His eyes popped out of his head. "You must be related to Adanma," he said. "I am friends with their family."

When I told him I had no idea who she was, he proceeded to introduce me to her. And that was how Adanma and I met.

Aside from our shared roots, we had lots of similar interests and commonalities. We became friends immediately, and she and her husband invited me over regularly. From our conversations, one could not tell that we'd recently met. I also found a local church and got connected. My relationship with Adanma, her family, and the church helped with my adjustment to the town. I began to settle in nicely and made the mental shift in a positive direction from loneliness to gratitude.

My phone rang again just when I was making peace with my reality. I had kept my interview appointment with the organization in Regina that called the day I was leaving Vancouver. Now I was being offered the job in Regina.

Standing here at this crossroads, I knew I had to decide whether to remain here or venture again into the unknown—Regina. My move to the town hadn't been as bad as I thought it would have been. New relationships. New environment. Learning what it's like to be me by spending considerable time with myself. But I had my employers to consider. They were patient with my slow decision-making process. It felt mean to walk out on them. My loyalty was at stake.

———————●———————

It was New Years Day. I sat in my bedroom overwhelmed with gratitude for my life—family, career, love. In that silent moment, I heard a voice, like a whisper in my ears.

"Osayi," the voice said, *"learn to forget the past and embrace the new beginning I have for you."*

I opened my eyes slowly, looked around my room and realized I was all alone. It felt so surreal, except that this was not the first time.

I can vividly remember the first time I heard this voice. It was before I left Vancouver. My friend and I had prayed together over the phone about my intended relocation. I was in public when her call came in, and I found a spot quiet enough for us to pray quickly.

We had just said our goodbyes when I heard a voice say, *"You are going to be alone with me."*

I looked around me, uncertain where the voice had originated. There was no one next to me. And even though others were standing nearby, they appeared to be in their own world, oblivious to my experience. I pushed the message aside, unable to decipher where it came from. Minutes later, the friend whom I had prayed with called back.

"I feel this strongly in my spirit concerning you, Osayi," she said. "I believe God wants you to be open to His plans for you."

Three months had gone by since that weird experience, and yet here I was in another province, having a similar experience, hearing a familiar whisper.

The day went by fast, and by evening, I began preparing for work the next day. I ironed my clothes, packed my lunch, unpacked and repacked my purse. In the midst of my busyness, I suddenly remembered that a close friend had not returned my call. Three days earlier, while we were having a conversation, she had to attend to "something urgent" that had come up. She promised to return my call soon.

"This is so not her," I thought. "Three days?"

I tried to reach her. My calls went unanswered. My text messages received no reply. A day had never gone by without her acknowledging my efforts to stay in touch.

"She is not answering my calls or responding to my messages," I said to Harry, agitatedly. "It is quite unusual for her to do so," I added.

He urged me to relax, and tried taking my mind off the fears that were beginning to creep in. "We just stepped into the new year. Maybe she needs time to unwind from all the planning, visiting, and cooking. Give her time, then reach out to her again," he said, making innocent excuses for her.

Still concerned about her wellbeing, I reached out to mutual friends who confirmed she was doing fine.

"Was she deliberately not taking my calls?" I wondered.

I ruminated on our most recent conversations; there was nothing alarming in them. I waited a few more days and, once again, reached out to her. No response. It was hard to believe at first. With no goodbyes, no explanations, my close friend had cut me off. I was hurt. I recounted moments when we encouraged each other through difficulties and laughed at each other's jokes. I was confused. Her actions made me feel tossed aside. Not understanding what had happened behind the scenes to influence the passive, all-in-your-face decision made the situation more unbearable for me. I was furious at the way she slammed the door with her silence, leaving me standing in the hallway. I missed her, so occasionally I'd knock on her door, only to have silence answer it.

I was awakened by a text alert on my phone at 3:00 a.m. I knew it would be one of my friends who resided either in Nigeria or the United Kingdom. Regardless of my frequent reminders of the different time zones and how that determines my availability, they always seemed to forget. With my eyelids half open, I struggled to read the text that had just come in. I was right. It was a message from a former classmate in Nigeria.

"Happy New Year! I thought of you today, and I believe God wants you to forget the past and embrace His plans for you. Read Isaiah 43:18-19," the text read.

The traditional New Year scripture, as I like to call it. Who does not quote or "claim" that scripture every start of the year? I shrugged it off, attaching no strings to the text message.

With her kids in bed and dinner already made, Adanma and I had enough time for our Friday evening small talk. I listened as she excitedly shared her plan for the New Year, which was to jump-start her career. I sat there, eagerly waiting for the right time to stylishly interrupt and share my ideas. The girl didn't give way, for sure.

"I am yet to decide if I will be moving to the city or remaining in this town," I said to her when, at last, she let me speak. Perplexed, I shared my experience with the voice I heard in Vancouver, here in Saskatchewan, and what friends had said to me.

We tried piecing the puzzle together, but it made no sense to us. Abandoning what we could not understand, we moved on to discussing the interests that connected us — self-development, spirituality, and empowerment.

Her husband returned from work and joined us in the living room immediately. He inquired about my decision to remain or relocate. When I told him how I was yet to decide, he gazed at me for a while and gently said, "Osayi, there is a new thing God wants to do in your life. Be alert, so you do not miss Him."

Adanma and I looked at each other in astonishment, and that was when I knew God was behind these messages. They were not just random.

———————●———————

I had four days left to get back to the employer in Regina, and I was still indecisive. Although I had asked my family, close friends, and even Harry what they thought, I wanted to own this career decision. I wanted to have no one to blame, but myself, should this turn out to be a wrong career move. And that was difficult for me. Then I realized I hadn't sought the counsel of the minister in the church I attended. So after service had ended on Sunday, I stayed behind to speak to him.

"I have no clue what I should do," I said to him, with confusion visibly expressed on my face.

"Would you like us to pray for direction?" he asked. After getting my consent, he beckoned two ladies in the lobby to join us. With eyes closed, the four of us held hands and prayed.

Right there and then, I felt the presence of someone else standing next to me. I opened my eyes to see who had joined us. It was still just the four of us. But still, I could sense the presence. It was overwhelming.

"Let us take a few minutes, be still in our spirits, and listen to what God has to say to us," instructed the minister, after we had all taken turns to pray.

I listened. I heard nothing. Like a sudden wave, thoughts about Israel's progress when they encountered the Red Sea began flooding my mind.

"Why am I thinking this? Of what relevance is it to my prayers?" I silently asked myself.

"Did God say something to you or impress anything on your spirit?" the minister asked, with his eyes fixed on me.

"Umm....no," I replied.

After a brief silence, he said, "As we prayed, the Lord said I should remind you of Israel and their progress at the River Jordan. He wants you to go forward, despite the obstacles."

I began piecing it all together. Those thoughts were not random. Israel at the Red Sea and River

With God, our progress is certain despite existing or future barriers.

Jordan happened at different seasons on their journey to Canaan but were symbolic of the same things—advancement despite visible barriers, their involvement in making progress, the death of the past, a new dawn, and God's omnipotence.

I dashed home after the prayer session. For the first time, I had a revelation of what Moses meant when he told Israel in the wilderness, *"For what great nation is there that has a god so near to it as the Lord our God is to us, whenever we call upon him?"* (Deuteronomy 4:7 ESV).

In the privacy of my home, I worshipped and prayed; anything to invite that presence again. My heart's cry for years has been to know God for myself, beyond the walls of the church and the lips of my ministers. Unpleasant life events had made me secretly, and sometimes openly, question God, His existence, and His love for me.

Hours later, I began to prepare myself mentally to move again. One of the things that had stood in my way of going to Regina was my inability to find accommodation. The fact that I was not physically present to check out the apartments also posed a barrier. No one will rent to someone they have not met in person. So I prayed, asking God to lead me and make a way.

After spending hours online in search of the perfect place, and long minutes on the phone with landlords and agents, who had either rented the space and still had the ads up or wanted to meet me to determine my suitability, I gave up. I was drained of energy, mentally and physically. To relax my mind and free it from worries, I took a break and decided to log on to Facebook. Not only would Facebook serve as a distraction from this search, but I'd also get to see what's new and exciting in the lives of my loved ones.

No sooner had I logged on to Facebook than a post appeared on my home page. Its words grabbed my attention. Kechi, a high school mate whom I had not seen since I graduated high school, had just updated her status, making comparisons between her sunshine experience during her visit to Nigeria and the excruciating winter that welcomed her in Regina.

"Regina!" I screamed in disbelief. "What's she doing in this place?"

I last saw her thirteen years ago in Nigeria. I wanted to reach out to her, but how do I reconnect with someone I have not spoken to in a while...I mean, years? Our paths regularly crossed, though we were not close friends in high school. It was a boarding school, so between the daily living experiences and student activities, Kechi and I knew each other well enough. We'd been friends on the giant social media platform for a while but barely checked on each other in real life. How sad.

Garnering courage, I sent her a message, asking if she was visiting Regina or lived there. Kechi's quick response was full of excitement to hear from me. When I informed her of my move, she wanted to know details of my relocation—where I'd be working and what my living arrangements were. She had lived there long enough and knew the ins and outs of the city.

"Wow!" she exclaimed. "Your office is situated just fifteen minutes away from my home."

"I will be going abroad for a one-year volunteer opportunity," she added. "You can sublet my fully furnished one-bedroom apartment, or if you find a place that interests you online, I could inspect it and give you valuable feedback."

I stared at my laptop screen in amazement.

Finally, Kechi said, "You could also live with me for a few days while you search for an apartment, in case you do not like mine."

All except the sublease were going to be at no cost.

My heart leaped for joy at the opportunities Kechi offered me, without me asking. Dealing and negotiating with prospective landlords and agents was an uneasy task, and here, someone offered willingly to do that for me. All I had been worried about worked out at the snap of a finger.

And that is how God made way for me. Ten days later, I arrived at Kechi's with my three bags and a large suitcase, ready for a new phase of my life in Regina.

Regina was a breath of fresh air. Gosh, I underestimated how much I missed the perks of city living—lights, noise, high-rise buildings, and easy access to the airport. Kechi's tastefully furnished apartment was right at the heart of Regina's downtown district. With the permission of her landlord, I sublet her apartment.

I was happy. I loved my new job. Its responsibilities were quite similar to my other job in Vancouver, but unique in its own way. In retrospect, I realized that the unpleasantness I felt in my job in Vancouver was never about the job. I needed that discomfort to stretch myself, learn new things, get out of my comfort zone, get new experiences, live life. Every day was different, and that was an added advantage for me. My relationship with Harry was growing steadily, and due to its proximity, I visited him regularly in Saskatoon.

Everything was right where they should be; right where I wanted them to be.

The ride was going on smoothly and peacefully, surrounded by lovely sights of mountains and trees on both sides. The path ahead of me was clear, and so I relaxed, savouring every moment of the journey, when suddenly, I hit a major bump. It was unexpected. There were no signposts on either side of the road to forewarn me of the dangers ahead. It was so fast that I could barely catch up with it. Everything seemed to be going south at the same time.

"Daddy will be alright," I endlessly encouraged myself as I sat on the plane headed to Vancouver to see my parents and siblings. Fond memories I had of my father weaved through my thoughts—his sacrifice, his courage, his love for us and others, his selflessness, his friendship. My sister, Mena said he was feeling unwell.

Worry and anxiety had become my companions ever since I was informed. Even though I had prayed, there still existed in me that deep, insatiable longing to be assured that all would be well. So I held out my hand to people that were dear to me. I needed to be encouraged. Only a few reached out to receive it. I was grateful for the few, even though it did not erase the hurt I felt from the silence and sudden absence of others I'd expected to be there.

Closing my eyes, I valiantly fought back the tears that arose and gathered in my eyes. My move to Regina had not only created a substantial gap between some of my friends and me, but also tore apart the friendship we once had. Though we stayed in touch often, things did not feel the same anymore. I could not explain the fall out, even if I tried, as I had initiated none of it. So I sat on the receiving end of these rejections.

The dust eventually settled. Daddy recovered fast and well. He said it was not serious, but my dad would never show it even if it was. I glued together the parts of myself that were ripped apart by these circumstances, reignited the engine of my life, and continued my life's journey with fewer people than at the beginning. This time, however, I moved at a pace slower than before. Never again did I want to arrive speedily at a bump I never foresaw. And I did see one coming, from Harry's infrequent calls to him becoming easily irritated.

I tried to turn a blind eye. The rejection and silence I had just dealt with had taken a toll on me emotionally, so I was reluctant to accept another invitation to trauma. At first, I denied its existence. But when it appeared glaringly before me, I gently slammed the brakes so the movement over this bump would be slower and safer than my last experience, and so I would feel less pain, less rejected. However, no matter how I tried, I still arrived there at breakneck speed.

I was drowning in confusion, pain, and anger. I am no stranger to self-doubt, rejection, and disappointment, but I certainly had not mastered the art of overcoming them. I knew just enough to numb myself to their pangs. Now I found myself on a path so unfamiliar—aloneness. My life had never been void of the sounds of laughter and endless phone conversations. The silence was deafening. Many I shared my bench with had gotten up and walked away, leaving me all by myself, including Harry.

With frequent weekend trips to Saskatoon, I barely had the time to build new relationships in Regina, and I became isolated. I was far, physically, from all my loved ones. But it was the emotional distance from many I was close to that pierced my heart the most. Their departure hurt, but the pain paled in comparison to the isolation I felt. Never in my life had I been stripped bare of the essence of myself.

Driven by the fear of loneliness, I opened myself up to people, regardless of how they treated me. I was transparent with them, sharing my dreams, strengths, fears, imperfections, wounds, and mistakes. With everyone that left, it felt like a piece of me had been ripped off and taken away, without my permission, and I could do nothing about it.

I began questioning and doubting my worth and esteem as I wondered deeply if I mattered to them. The more I did this, the more it felt like a scab in my heart was being forcefully peeled off, exposing deep emotional wounds that needed a long time to heal. I had no clue how lost and vulnerable I had become, until my relationship with Harry ended. It took that to see that I was no longer recognizable. Between the desire to please him at all costs and maintain my popularity with friends, I lost someone vital—me. The *me* who was unashamed to laugh freely in public; unafraid to use my voice; bold enough to speak my truth, even when it was unpopular; open enough to let people know me. I missed that me. This quirkiness made me *me*. All that was gone. I had immersed myself so deeply in people-pleasing that even my confidence to regain my independence was completely lost.

Worse, I was all by myself—an unexplored territory for me. Sometimes, we find it hard to let go of the things, people, and habits that hurt us, because it is easier for us to deal with their presence (our comfort zone) than their absence, for fear of what we will be without them.

I wanted to speak to someone in person, cry with someone, vent my emotions to anyone. If there was ever a time when I needed company, it was now. I had no one in Regina. Lara tried to be there for me the best way she could, but she was far away in Saskatoon. She wanted me to have a fresh perspective on the whirlwind of experiences.

Wiping away the tears that streamed down my face, I slowly picked up my cell phone that was on the centre table to reach out to my friend, Rose. She had always understood my unspoken words and knew how to interpret, often accurately, my meaningless gestures and deep sighs. But I was afraid, afraid of me, the common denominator in everything that had taken place.

"Will she cast me off as well?" I struggled within myself to answer that question.

Still, I reached out. It was midnight where Rose lived, but I decided to give it a try.

"Hello, Rose," I whispered the moment I heard her at the receiving end, my voice shaky at the mere possibility of her tossing me aside like the others.

Immediately, I could tell the poor self-esteem and self-worth issues I had neatly tucked away years ago were gradually rearing their ugly heads.

"It's so sweet to hear from you, Osayi. Shouldn't you be in bed?" asked Rose. "What's going on?"

I sighed. For minutes, we both said nothing. I never had to utter a word for Rose to hear my heart speak. Without sharing details, she knew exactly what to do.

"You should listen to this," she said, breaking the silence as she pulled her laptop closer to her phone and began playing a gospel song I had never heard before.

Again, I felt that presence like I did the other day in church. This time around, it was more comforting and reassuring than over-whelming. An hour later, I was awoken by the sound of music in my bedroom. I was frightened, until I realized I had fallen asleep while listening to the song Rose was playing on her laptop. I felt bad that I had dozed off on her, she who was kind enough to take my call when she did.

"Rose?" I called out her name, expecting no response.

"Hey, you are awake," she said, cutting me short as I tried to apologize for falling asleep. She lovingly continued, "I knew you had fallen asleep, but I decided to stay up just to be sure you are okay before I go to bed."

It was now 2:00 a.m. where she lived.

I cried again, this time at the blessing of having a friend like Rose. She was indeed a friend. I had not been more loving towards her than those I could no longer find by my side.

———————◆———————

I was determined to embrace these surprises that sprung on my path but found no strength within me to drive forward. It took a lot of courage that I certainly did not have, not at this time. The sting of aloneness began to hurt more, and I was not enjoying any bit of it. Every passing moment was a constant reminder that I was unseen, insignificant, forgotten, and lost.

The sound of my phone ringing jolted me to my senses. I suspected the caller was either my parents or my siblings.

"My dear, are you okay?" my mother asked after I hit the green button.

Amidst sniffles, I responded that I was doing well.

"Daddy and I want to remind you of our love for you," she said reassuringly. "I know you are going through a trying time with everything that has come your way. You never know why these things happen, but I want you to hold your head high through this."

What was meant to encourage me became the catalyst for another bout of tears. My parents stayed on the phone with me until they felt I was alright. Then we said our goodbyes.

The day was still young and bright that Tuesday. It was some-where around 6:20 p.m., but I wanted to retire early to bed. I was about to turn off my cell phone when I heard the voice tell me, *"Do not turn off your phone yet."*

I had lived in that apartment for months now, and the last time I checked, I lived alone. Standing up from the couch where I laid, I walked into my bedroom and bathroom to be sure there was no one else inside. There certainly was no one. I went back to my couch, a little afraid.

"I am not going crazy, am I?" I asked myself. I picked up my phone from where I'd left it and attempted to turn it off.

Immediately, the voice reminded me about a friend's church I had attended years ago when I visited her in Winnipeg, a major city in the province of Manitoba. Having become hooked on the min-ister's style of preaching and powerful words of encouragement, I frequently streamed their services online or listened to their pod-casts whenever I needed encouragement.

"I want you to listen attentively to the message preached tonight at this church," the voice added.

I was too downcast to hear any message, but I obeyed this subtle voice giving me directions. I disconnected my laptop from its charger, and visited the church's website, where services are regularly live-streamed on service days. From what I could recall, the timing was spot-on for their weekly Tuesday services. Thus, I was surprised that evening when I visited their site and saw that the service would not be available via streaming.

"My mind must have made this all up," I concluded, tossing my laptop aside and hitting the button to turn off my phone so I could sleep.

The voice, though gentle, was now firm, *"Osayi, I told you not to turn off your cell. I did not ask you to stream the message online. I have spoken to Teanna to call you so you can listen to it through her phone."*

Two minutes later, my phone rang. It was Teanna. Teanna is the friend I accompanied to church when I visited Winnipeg.

"Osayi, my church minister just entered the pulpit to preach, and I heard the Holy Spirit tell me to call you so you can listen to it," said Teanna amidst the sound of singing and clapping in her background.

"The Holy Spirit? Could this be Him?" I pondered, processing all that had taken place within the last ten minutes—the timing of Teanna's call, as I sat on the edge of my seat waiting because the voice had asked me to. Every other experience I had had so far could have been a coincidence. The cab driver who showed up at a time I needed that support, a coincidence. The Red Sea and River Jordan stories with the minister in the town at our prayer time, a bigger coincidence. But this was too precise to be happenstance.

Gladdened that my mind was not playing tricks on me, I sat still, though puzzled, through the forty minutes of teaching. In the many words spoken, one of the Bible verses that framed the message kept replaying in my head. *"That I may know him and the power of his resurrection, and may share his sufferings, becoming like him in his death, that by any means possible I may attain the resurrection from the dead"* (Philippians 3:10-11 ESV).

Paul, having faced many hardships, and currently imprisoned, had one great desire—to know God. In a place of uneasiness and discomfort, all Paul wanted was to know God more.

"What exactly does knowing God have to do with my situation?" I asked myself as I listened wholeheartedly to the sermon through Teanna's phone. "How else am I supposed to know Him that I don't already?"

I was not a new Christian. I have been a church-goer for most of my life, even at times when I did not know why. It was a religious activity for me. Occasionally, I drifted, only to find myself back again after life had tossed me to and fro. In the most recent years, I began to know my "why" for going. I loved God. He had to be the One who strengthened me on days I wanted to give up.

Although I did not fully understand what was happening in my life, I was happy. God cared about me so much that he called my attention to a sermon focused on Paul's isolation in Rome and how he made the best of it. In that place, he wrote letters to the different churches, and these letters are now a part of the New Testament. I did not know there was a difference between serving God and knowing God. One can serve God without knowing Him, but it is in the *knowing* Him that our service becomes meaningful, not merely a religious ritual but an intentional act of love towards someone we know intimately. With this love comes a deep sense of devotion to Him.

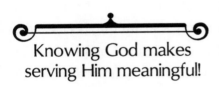

Knowing God makes serving Him meaningful!

I learned through the preaching that my struggle, challenges, and hurts served a purpose. It did not matter how I got here, mentally, emotionally, and spiritually. What was important was what I did here. Like Paul in isolation, could I seize this opportunity to know God more? Could I see the advantage in what looked like a disadvantage?

Teanna and I chatted briefly as soon as the service ended. It was fascinating to see how one could be stranded somewhere and God sends help from another part of the world. He sent help to renew my perspective on my situation and as a perfect reminder that I am never out of His reach as His child. It was still a blur to me, but I remembered the words I had heard months before, "*You are going to be alone...with me.*"

Here I was, alone with this voice that spoke to me and talked back to me sometimes. It was not what I envisioned. I still wondered how I would navigate my life and this season without the support of people, without the encouragement of those whose applause I craved. God's presence should have been enough for me, but I still wondered. I held

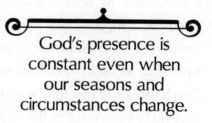

God's presence is constant even when our seasons and circumstances change.

on dearly to the validations of people, and now in their absence, despite God's presence, I still felt like a fish pulled out from the water and left to die on the shore.

It was a new day, but the message from the night before was still fresh on my mind. I highly anticipated the availability of the message podcast on their website so I could listen to it, again. That morning I opened a message I'd received from a former colleague in Vancouver who was not privy to my personal life, I realized he had sent me the link to a YouTube video. He captioned it, "God wants you to watch this."

The preacher in the video was sharing details of his life, including a time when he questioned God's presence in the unpleasant circumstances of his life. He thought God didn't love or care for him, but when he allowed God to walk with him, work in him, and work through him, he was able to testify that he knows God, as written in Philippians 3:10.

My eyes began to well up with tears of gratitude. God was communicating that Scripture to me, again. I could not ignore the writing on the wall. Garnering strength, I rose from the couch, walked into my bedroom and returned with my Bible, pen, and a journal. I flipped open the Bible to Philippians 3:10 and prayed amidst tears, "God, I want to know You and the power of your resurrection. Reveal yourself to me like You have never done before. Teach me. Lead me. Stay with me. Speak to me in ways that I will recognize your voice in the midst of mine, others', and the devil's, in Jesus' name. Amen."

Chapter Three

UNWRAPPED

"The unfolding of your words gives light; it gives understanding to the simple" (Psalm 119:130 NIV).

ONE OF THE items I purchased in Regina, after my car, was a Global Positioning System (GPS). As a newbie, there was no way I could drive to the office without knowing how to navigate my way there. The GPS, however, was created for such a time as this. I was confident that whenever I entered any address, it would undoubtedly lead me to it. That was until the day my most reliable means of direction led me to a major bus depot, instead of the hospital where I was to attend a meeting. With blind trust, I followed its instructions, confident that it knew the route to get me to my destination. The stares from the depot employees quickly made me realize that my beloved GPS had failed me.

How does one make their way through new territories, physically, spiritually, emotionally, academically, and professionally, without a guide? We all need one. Tour guides earn a living for this reason. They know the ins and outs of the places we desire to go and have recent updates on information we seek to learn within their area of expertise. Scripture also teaches that to ask for guidance on roads we have less travelled gives us rest. However, we have a choice to follow the directions or not. *"This is what the Lord says: 'Stand at the crossroads and look; ask for the ancient paths, ask where the good way is, and walk in it, and you will find rest for your souls.' But you said, 'We will not walk in it'"* (Jeremiah 6:16 NIV).

What do you do when you stand at the crossroads and there is no one to ask for the "ancient paths?" What do you do when those you meet there as clueless as you are? To go where one has never travelled before requires the leading of one who has, or one who knows the way. I may have found myself in uncharted territories before, but never have I found myself alone, physically,

> To go where one has never travelled before requires the leading of one who has, or one who knows the way.

emotionally, and spiritually. How do I navigate this? To the best of my understanding, those who had my best interest at heart had never felt this abandoned before. Thus, my family and friends who stood by me were there for me but could not understand the feelings I struggled with or the lens through which I defined my experience. How could they lead me out of the dejection, loneliness, and self-pity I felt when they had never been there before?

It was Sunday morning, and I was yet to decide what church I would be attending that day. I had churches I visited whenever I stayed in Regina for the weekend and did not travel to Saskatoon.

The morning was still early, giving me enough time to do my morning devotion. As I flipped to the next page of my Bible to continue reading from where I last stopped in Jeremiah, I realized I had read its final chapter. The next book, chronologically, is Lamentations. Between the books of Lamentations, Ezekiel, and Revelation in the Bible, I cannot tell which one I avoid reading the most. I found the first two books sorrowful and the latter terrifying. Often, I would skim through the chapters, and sometimes skip the entire book.

With the current events in my life, I wanted to read something more comforting like the Psalms, not Lamentations. As I proceeded to carry out my actions, a still, small voice spoke again, loud enough for me not to miss it.

"I want you to read the Book of Lamentations, and I will walk you through it."

Drowning out many voices in my life made it easier for me to recognize this voice when it spoke. I could even hear my thoughts.

Jeremiah, the writer of Lamentations, was utterly broken as he described in the first chapter the state of Jerusalem, once occupied, and now deserted. The people were hurting with no one to comfort them. I could totally plug myself into those verses and fit right in. It was at Lamentations 3:21 that my reading climaxed. The light at the tunnel's end was right there. Pain-alleviating, life-giving, and soul-soothing words penned in a book that started off in despair. It felt like beauty born out of ugly situations, sure hope that terrible times don't always last. *"But this I call to mind, and therefore I have hope: The steadfast love of the Lord never ceases; his mercies never come to an end; they are new every morning; great is your faithfulness. 'The Lord is my portion,' says my soul, 'therefore I will hope in him'"* (Lamentations 3:21-24 ESV).

"Pause, Osayi," I heard the voice instruct me. *"Don't rush through that. I want you to read those verses carefully."*

I understood, as I continued my study of these verses, the permanence of God's love, kindness, and compassion. Who else to place our hope and trust in than One whose love is ever sure?

> Thankfulness has nothing to do with the situation, but everything to do with my perspective on the situation.

Still on the borderline between attending a Sunday service or not, I picked up my laptop to connect online to my friend's church in Winnipeg. This time around, the message was live-streamed. I was right on time to hear the preacher begin his sermon from Lamentations 3:21-24. I listened with keen interest as he discussed it further. Though he reiterated things I had just learned from my personal study minutes earlier, he had an interesting insight, one I could never have imagined from the pages of Lamentations — gratitude.

If you have ever found yourself in circumstances where you feel misunderstood, deserted, and fearful, gratitude is not what immediately comes to mind. How does one express thanks when loved ones walk away? Or, devastatingly, when they die? Who wears dancing shoes when they have just lost their source of livelihood? Then it struck me that I could not be hopeful if I was not thankful. Thankfulness has nothing to do with the situation, but everything to do with my perspective on the situation. And to get the right perspective of a glaringly painful condition is an uneasy task. How do we see God in the backdrop of the events, pleasant or sad, that unfold in our lives?

Interrupting my thoughts, the voice said, *"I have heard your prayer asking me to lead you to a local church where you can develop more in the faith. I led you there. You attended once and never went back."*

"You led me? Where?" I asked. I received a response almost immediately. I recalled the first and only time I attended the church the voice brought to my mind. The preacher's message was timely for me, and the members had a strong sense of community that was very apparent on that first visit. I had no genuine reason for not returning, except I still needed to pray about that decision while shopping around for other options.

"It is not too late, Osayi. You can make it on time for service today," the voice encouraged me.

I hurriedly got ready and stepped out, all dressed for church that Sunday morning.

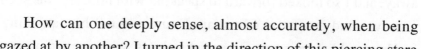

How can one deeply sense, almost accurately, when being gazed at by another? I turned in the direction of this piercing stare and my eyes locked with hers. I almost screamed out loudly. I was full of excitement at the mere sight of an old friend I knew back in Vancouver. I was surprised, as she was not at this church when I last visited.

Walking up to me at the end of the service, she asked in astonishment, "What are you doing here? I never expected to run into you, again."

We spent a considerable amount of time catching up with one another. Although my friend was only here briefly to visit family, it felt so good to hang around someone familiar. I knew God had led me to this church, not only to reconnect with an old friend, but to be committed in my service to Him and others in this place.

For every thirty minutes that I took my eyes away from the clock, it turned out to be only five minutes in reality. Five minutes. The time could not move any slower. With the way it was going, it could take two days to arrive at 5:00 p.m. The excitement of catching up with Ali, a distant relative, was so overwhelming I could barely wait to call it a day from work.

Ali's move to Regina was, in my opinion, divinely orchestrated. He had recently started working on a business project here in Regina four days a week. We sometimes hung out whenever he was here. As was his custom, he returned home to be with his family in Montreal every Saturday. For weeks now, he had been away, and I so looked forward to speaking with him. He was such a mature and insightful Christian. You could tell him anything, and he would always have powerful insights, without making you feel belittled or condemned. So Ali sat, listening to me vent about everything going on in my life. I was broken and confused. Ali, on the other hand, wore a smile on his lips that did not seem to complement the stories I was sharing with him.

"Why are you here?" he asked.

"Here?" I replied in bewilderment, as I was taken aback by his question.

"Why are you here in Regina?" he asked again.

Unsure of the question, or rather the intent of the question, I stayed mute.

"Have you heard of the person of the Holy Spirit?" Ali asked me rhetorically.

I nodded affirmatively.

"It is not just God speaking to you. It is His Spirit, the Holy Spirit, talking to you. If you continue to seek God's face in the midst of everything, He will guide you and give you clarity. So pray and be conscious of His presence with you. Invite Him in your personal Bible reading and your prayer time. Don't be eager to get up and leave right after you have prayed. Wait expectantly for Him to speak to you," Ali advised.

I did not show up in this city expecting to have my life turned upside down. I came ready to live the city life to which I was accustomed. Since I arrived in Saskatchewan, even while in the small town, I realized my desires were totally out of shape. My craving to spend time reading the Bible, the Word of God intensified to the point of worry. It became my companion and went everywhere with me—the car, the grocery store, the bed, and even at dinner time. I was not making sense to myself anymore. Little did I know that God had turned my desires to prepare me for the season I was about to enter.

Proverbs 21:1 tells us that *"The king's heart is a stream of water in the hand of the Lord; he turns it wherever he will"* (ESV). Some scriptures I had previously studied came alive in my spirit whenever I felt the pangs of rejection and aloneness afresh, like I did one evening when I got back home from work. There existed within me an emptiness that even Ali's wisdom-filled and comforting words could not fill. Ali's words did me a lot of good, but I was still insatiable. Ali's presence, though a constant reminder of God's faithfulness to send me help, did not end my confusion but helped me see this season differently.

I brought out my journal, in which I had penned scriptures months earlier, and saw this:

"Fear not, for I am with you; be not dismayed, for I am your God; I will strengthen you, I will help you, I will uphold you with my righteous right hand" (Isaiah 41:10 ESV). Tears poured from my eyes as I read and meditated on that verse. Months earlier, it was just a random verse that kept replaying in my mind. Today, I desperately needed to experience the truth and realness in those words. My knees gave way as I fell to the ground, praying for God to show me how this scripture applied to me. I fell asleep in that uncomfortable position.

It was past midnight when I awoke and dragged my body, stiffened by pain, to the bedroom. On the bed laid my cell phone, blinking to catch my attention and alert me of updates. I realized, upon looking at it, that I had received my devotion for the day. The writer of this devotional had in that day's piece sliced Isaiah 41:10 into digestible bits that I could relate to and understand. God saw my heart and knew how much I desired to learn about this verse. It was timely, and its lessons practical.

If you are in the wilderness today, be confident that God is right there with you. No matter the depth of your emotional, spiritual, or financial desert, be assured of one thing—God is right there with you. You can bank on His presence, for He is faithful. His presence guides us, provides when our financial flow ceases, comforts when the tears keep running, makes a way and creates opportunities when we have lost every flicker of hope. Before we ever feel alone, God is already there, awaiting us.

———————◆———————

It was time to get dressed. I knew where every single item I needed to adorn myself was. Picking up my pen, I wrote out the words, constantly cross-checking with my Bible to ensure that I had written the verses accurately. I needed this sword sharp. My outfit was biblical and exactly what was needed to fight against the scary dream that had just deprived me of a sweet night's rest. I got dressed, following the fashion steps outlined in Ephesians 6:10-18.

"Finally, be strong in the Lord and in the strength of his might. Put on the whole armor of God, that you may be able to stand against the schemes of the devil. For we do not wrestle against flesh and blood, but against the rulers, against the authorities, against the cosmic powers over this present darkness, against the spiritual forces of evil in the heavenly places. Therefore take up the whole armor of God, that you may be able to withstand in the evil day, and having done all, to stand firm. Stand therefore, having fastened on the belt of truth, and having put on the breastplate of righteousness, and, as shoes for your feet, having put on the readiness given by the gospel of peace. In all circumstances take up the

shield of faith, with which you can extinguish all the flaming darts of the evil one; and take the helmet of salvation, and the sword of the Spirit, which is the word of God, praying at all times in the Spirit, with all prayer and supplication. To that end, keep alert with all perseverance, making supplication for all the saints" (ESV).

I had woken up suddenly from a dream, panting heavily, as though a raging bull had been chasing me. I was in the midst of people familiar to me. We stood together, chatting and having fun. An intruder showed up, interrupting our gathering. I heard the intruder call out my name, "Osayi!" Reluctantly, I walked up to him, only to hear him ask for my undivided attention. Here he was, a complete stranger, making such a massive demand.

"But I...I want to be with them," I responded, feeling very upset. Ignoring him, I turned around and returned to my circle. To my surprise, one by one, as I resumed conversations with them, they began turning their backs on me. I stood there, crying.

"Osayi!" I heard him call, again.

Then I opened my eyes.

Dreams where your name is called out or you see yourself with animals have a negative connotation in the cultural environment in which I was raised. Such dreams are not to be toyed with, and so, for the life of me, I could not let this slide. I began to pray. I did not know the person, and I certainly didn't want him around me or calling my name. Every break I got from my regular activities, I spent time praying and reading the Word. It was my safe place.

Days later, I arrived at the book of John, following my personal Bible study guideline. I had no idea how engrossed and lost I was in its pages until I arrived at the fifteenth chapter way earlier than expected. In His lifetime, Jesus used lots of metaphors to illustrate

His points when teaching the disciples and the multitude that often surrounded Him. Of all the teachings, the most intriguing to me were the benefits of clinging to Jesus in John 15. My eyes slowly scanned the words written in this chapter as I reveled in their truth. I understood from that chapter that the degree at which Jesus is reflected in me, and through me, is dependent on my proximity to Him. *"You did not choose me. I chose you..."* My heartstrings pulled when I read these words in verse 16.

As I meditated on those lines in verse 16, I realized that to be selected was to be picked out from other options. Having a single item leaves you with no options for selection. Jesus had options. Do you have any idea how many people flocked around Him when He spoke? There were thousands. But Jesus carefully handpicked His twelve disciples, each with a unique destiny to fulfill. None that He chose frowned upon His decision. Instead, the Bible records that some left all they had known—businesses, careers, and even people—and just followed Him. Why would they act in such a manner?

The disciples knew the joy of being the Master's choice. They understood that being chosen meant a separation from the crowd. It all depends on how and what one sees. The disciples could have chosen to focus on what they missed by not being in the multitude, but in reality their separation made them understand how blessed they were to be a part of His plan. The enemy would like you and me to focus more on our separation from people, possessions, and places to distract us from paying attention to the "why" behind it. We quickly buy and accept the lies of man's exclusion more than the truth of God's inclusion, because we crave human acceptance and approval. So, rather than rejoice when God calls us, we cry, whine, and become bitter when people or possessions leave us, unaware that their absence creates the perfect environment to answer God's call. We have a choice to either go by how we feel about our circumstance, or go by what God's Word says about the situation. God sure had a way of giving me *aha* moments. Minutes later, I received an article from a friend and a devotional in my email on John 15:16. "*You have not chosen Me, but I have chosen you and I have appointed and placed and purposefully planted you, so that you would go and bear fruit and keep on bearing, and that your fruit will remain and be lasting, so that whatever you ask of the Father in My name [as My representative] He may give to you*" (John 15: 16 AMP). Both writers shared personal stories of God teaching them about His presence in seasons where they felt abandoned, and of accomplishing His purpose in their lives. Like me, they needed to see from His perspective before comprehending the beauty and lessons of this season.

> We have a choice to either go by how we feel about our circumstance, or go by what God's Word says about the situation.

Being guided to study the Bible and receiving the stories when I did were enough proof of God's presence and interest in my affairs. It increased my faith in Him for new and rewarding relationships, a new chapter, fresher revelations of Him, and His companionship.

I remembered that Ali had called me months earlier, after I felt deserted.

"I have been praying for you," he said. "God told me to share these two scriptures with you."

I grabbed my pen and journal, positioning my fingers to write these encouraging scriptures.

"2 Corinthians 1:3-4," he stated.

"Corinthians?" I muttered under my breath, as I wondered what words of encouragement existed within its pages. When I opened the Bible, I burst into a fresh bout of tears. *"Blessed be the God and Father of our Lord Jesus Christ, the Father of mercies and God of all comfort, who comforts us in all our affliction, so that we may be able to comfort those who are in any affliction, with the comfort with which we ourselves are comforted by God"* (2 Corinthians 1:3-4 ESV).

"Comfort," I said repeatedly. "Does this mean I am going to be in this hurt for a while and be comforted?" It was too painful to imagine. "Can I just not have this happen to me?" Heartbreaks, betrayals, disappointments, and personal failures, though difficult, were, in my opinion, easier to handle than feeling abandoned.

"The second one..." Ali continued.

I sat in eager expectation to hear what he wanted to share with me.

"2 Corinthians 6:17a - *'Therefore go out from their midst, and be separate from them, says the Lord'"* (ESV).

I remembered how fuzzy I was the day he shared those verses with me. I couldn't ascertain how they related to me. Now I had a clearer understanding that God could pass any message across to anyone from any page of His Word, because *"All Scripture is God-breathed and is useful for teaching, rebuking, correcting and training in righteousness"* (2 Timothy 3:16 NIV). He could breathe life and give meaning to a scripture so it is in ways applicable to my experience. The puzzle pieces were finally coming together, from the scriptures Ali had shared with me to the dream and the word in John 15:16. They all pointed in the same direction; I had been drafted into God's plan for my life, not cast aside by others. I was picked out and not put down.

This season was here to play a role in my life's bigger picture; a role I may not fathom now. My response to this challenge could either keep me stuck in anger and unforgiveness or cause me to go forward. So, I braced myself, ready to soak it all in — roses, purpose, and thorns.

Chapter Four

UNLIKELY BLESSING

"So Jacob was left alone, and a man wrestled with him till daybreak" (Genesis 32:24 NIV).

PERSPECTIVE CHANGES EVERYTHING.

"How could she just sit there and leave all the work to me?" a lady mumbled to herself about her sister. She stood by the door, waving her arms back and forth to grab her sister's attention to come into the kitchen where she belonged. Seeing that her tactics brought no result, she peeked around the corner, throwing a glance her way to indicate that she needed her help. Still, her sister just sat there. Her eyes, mind, heart, soul, and spirit all focused on Him. The "Him" in the living room.

To one, He was her Lord. Her Lord, in the same space with her. Nothing else mattered, and her demeanour proved it. To the other, even though she called Him 'Lord,' she saw and treated Him as a guest she needed to cater to. One man, two different viewpoints, and reactions to His presence.

"Now as they went on their way, Jesus entered a village. And a woman named Martha welcomed him into her house. And she had a sister called Mary, who sat at the Lord's feet and listened

to his teaching. But Martha was distracted with much serving. And she went up to him and said, 'Lord, do you not care that my sister has left me to serve alone? Tell her then to help me.' But the Lord answered her, 'Martha, Martha, you are anxious and troubled about many things, but one thing is necessary. Mary has chosen the good portion, which will not be taken away from her'" (Luke 10:38-42 ESV).

Jesus ministered to Mary. Intimacy flowed between them as she sat, humbled, at His feet, paying attention to His every word. On the flip side was her sister, Martha, ministering to her assumption of Jesus' needs. She was certainly not wrong. Yet, she was not right either. Here, in her living room, was a man whose attention the crowd craved. His teachings, His provision, His mercy, and His saving power made Him a life changer.

Imagine Jesus in the flesh seated in your home. Whom would you rather be, Mary or Martha? The one who understands how much she needs Jesus or the one who tries to prove herself to Jesus, forgetting that He loved her long before she deserved it? The one who willingly puts aside anything that can compete with His presence or the one who attempts to juggle everything at the same time, including His presence? We often try to prove ourselves to Jesus, forgetting He loved us long before we deserved it.

"One thing is necessary," Jesus told Martha (Luke 10:42 ESV).

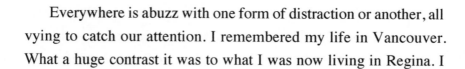

Everywhere is abuzz with one form of distraction or another, all vying to catch our attention. I remembered my life in Vancouver. What a huge contrast it was to what I was now living in Regina. I felt like two different people. In Vancouver, I went to work and attended services in church regularly on weekdays. But my evenings and weekends were filled with one activity or the other. There was someone getting married, having a baby, moving into a new apartment, buying a house, or some other celebration that took place for no reason at all. Each of these milestones came with a minimum of

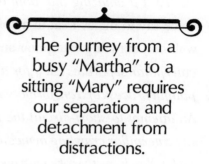

The journey from a busy "Martha" to a sitting "Mary" requires our separation and detachment from distractions.

one celebratory event. Some had more than one event. For many of them, I was not only a guest but also fully immersed in the event planning. I was Martha.

The journey from "Martha" to "Mary" is one Google Maps cannot give directions for. It requires separation from what catches our interest the most and detachment from what competes for our attention, causing us to zero in on what is most important. Distractions are not always the big things that steal our focus off what is important. Even good things can be distractions, if they are not what we are meant to be doing at that time.

Outlook matters. When the people or circumstances that define or characterize a "Martha" are stripped off her, she does not immediately see a "Mary" in the making. Instead, she sees loss of self and identity, fear of what could be, vulnerability, anger, rejection, and disappointment. That was how I felt. When I heard, *"You are going to be alone...with me"* months earlier, I was oblivious to the cost of journeying from a busy Martha to a sitting Mary. I had to experience these disappointments to attend this appointment with Him. What appeared on the surface level as a rejection was a rerouting to God.

———————◉———————

"Isn't it amazing that both are the same creature?" I heard the voice say to me as I sat in a coffee shop, admiring a picture on the wall of a crawling caterpillar and a beautiful winged butterfly. *"The caterpillar separates itself for a time from others and undergoes the painful process of transformation to become what it was created to be. An attempt to short-circuit the process or avoid the process leaves the caterpillar crawling in mediocrity or living as a dysfunctional butterfly. You have to work with me willingly, and this season will not be long. I will teach you what the Bible has to say about transformation when you get home,"* the voice said conclusively.

I quickly scribbled on a piece of paper what I heard.

In the comfort of my home, I read more about the caterpillar, the chrysalis it spins around itself for seclusion, the transformation that happens within the chrysalis, and the butterfly that finally emerges. To the one looking from the outside, nothing significant is going on there. It is just a place of stillness. However, within the chrysalis, a noticeable change is happening.

If only Martha knew how much was poured into Mary as she sat still and undisturbed at Jesus' feet, she would have put her serving hat away. The death of their brother revealed how dissimilar they were in their relationship with Jesus. Mary sat in the house until Jesus sent for her through Martha, who had earlier dashed out to meet Him, filled with complaints regarding His late arrival. When Mary came based on His invitation, she fell again at His feet. There were memories at this place of stillness. In this lowly position, she had learned from Him. Here, she had cleaned His feet, drying it with her hair. Her body language seemed to echo, even in her saddened state, "Lord, the same place I sat to learn from you is where I am pouring out my heart to you. Your love for me won't let You leave me in this state. Lord, do something!"

Her presence and tears moved Jesus. It was evident that with her quietness and humility came an internal change that was displayed by her response to Jesus in spite of this tragedy. It is captivating to see that the caterpillar could successfully transform into a butterfly inside the chrysalis and still not reach its highest potential. The butterfly struggles to come out of the chrysalis, and that fight itself serves a purpose in strengthening its wings to fly. Any Good Samaritan attempt to help break it free would be more disastrous to its future as a butterfly than helpful.

That evening, I turned to Romans 12 to study what it had to say on transformation. *"Do not conform to the pattern of this world, but be transformed by the renewing of your mind. Then you will be able to test and approve what God's will is—his good, pleasing and perfect will"*(Romans 12:2 NIV). Conform? Transform? I pondered these words. As I did, my mind opened up like flower petals, expanding my understanding.

Conforming keeps us in alignment with others and makes us the same as everyone else. We get lost in the crowd and fail to be distinct. On the other hand, embracing and celebrating our uniqueness brings us recognition. The key to unlocking this peculiarity is transformation; seeing, thinking, and understanding differently. The change brought by transformation causes us to stand out from others. Thoughts began to flood my mind as I went on meditating on

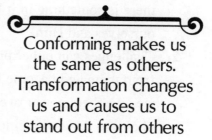

Conforming makes us the same as others. Transformation changes us and causes us to stand out from others

that verse.

After a long evening, I pulled up my sheets and slid myself in, ready for a good night's sleep.

———————◆———————

The rays of early morning light piercing through my bedroom curtains and resting on my face did a better job than my alarm in getting me out of bed. Minutes later, I proceeded to read my daily devotional, so I could fully start my day. It was Saturday, and I had plans to enjoy the sunlight since the fall season was fast approaching. Surprisingly, my devotional that morning was on the butterfly and the painful process of transformation that leads to this beautiful work of art. The writer used stories of biblical heroes who, through the challenges God permitted them to experience, became like the butterfly — stronger and more resilient, because they embraced the process of transformation.

If anything, I could see God driving home how serious He wanted me to take this season. So I relaxed more, giving myself time to meditate on change and identify more with the butterfly. As I did this, I realized that:

1. God does not cause evil, but when He allows a situation, there is something in it for us to learn and discover about ourselves and Him.
2. Challenges can either bring out the best in us, if we learn from them and become better, or reveal the worst in us, if we give them power over us and become bitter. We have a choice to decide the impact challenges have on us.

3. Acknowledging the lessons learned can make us. Avoiding them can break us, because life will take us through the challenge all over again until we get recognize the lessons.

4. We could get distracted and end the process of transformation before its work is complete, and come out unprepared and underdeveloped. Or we could endure the season and process, and emerge as the butterfly in full strength, beauty, and glory.

5. Challenges come and go, and were never meant to be permanent or a symbol of our identity. Instead, they help to build our character and strengthen us.

6. The cycle of transformation does not come to an end because we keep transforming into Christ's image until we depart from this earth. This continuous transformation builds character in us, matures us, prepares us for greater works ahead, and molds us. It means we should be better today than we were yesterday as long as we keep walking with God and allowing Him to work in us and through us. 2 Corinthians 3: 18 (AMP) describes this: *"And we all, with unveiled face, continually seeing as in a mirror the glory of the Lord, are progressively being transformed into His image from [one degree of] glory to [even more] glory, which comes from the Lord, [who is] the Spirit."*

If we cut short the process of transformation, either by leaving the Christian faith, or continuing in the faith without investing time in maintaining our relationship with God by studying the Bible, prayer, and fellowshipping with other Christians, we become like the dysfunctional butterfly with wings that cannot fly.

———————●———————

"For by the grace given me I say to every one of you: Do not think of yourself more highly than you ought, but rather think of yourself with sober judgment, in accordance with the faith God has distributed to each of you" (Romans 12:3 NIV).

"I don't understand what this verse means," I said aloud to myself as I continued studying the book of Romans. Cognizant that I was not alone, I began reading the Scriptures with an expectation to be taught what I could not comprehend by the One who speaks to me.

"I want you to reflect on your life. Are you where you ought to be? Do you know who you are and whose you are?" I heard the voice ask me.

I was silent.

"Look inwards, Osayi. Think of your life's journey and experiences to this point. How have they shaped you? You allowed the positive experiences to make you prideful. You used the negatives— your failures, struggles, and disappointments—to define yourself. You are not living up to my expectation of you.

"Burdens. You are carrying so much hurt, pain, anger, and unforgiveness. You are stuck and cannot move with these anymore. It is pride to think you are able enough to handle these without me. Do not think that much of yourself."

By this time, I was moved to tears. I felt a volcanic eruption within me as memories I had suppressed and hidden for so long suddenly resurfaced. The curtain I used to cover up wounds and baggage was suddenly pulled back, revealing issues I had avoided dealing with for a long time.

"You will have to walk through those memories, Osayi."

"No!" I said, amidst burning tears.

"I will walk with you. I will help you let go of the past so you can embrace the future I have for you. You need me."

It was a painful realization to come to terms with. I knew I needed help. Over the years, I saw my once-confident self gradually become a shadow of what I used to be. With every blow life gave me, I became bent over, unable to stand up to its challenges. I read books. I got counselling. These things work, as many have received their healing and deliverance from them. But not me. And I did not know why. So, I kept up the façade, bracing myself to face the world while I bled on the inside.

All his life, he always got what he wanted. He could quickly wiggle out of any problem, but here he was, trapped between a brother seeking revenge for his deceitfulness and betrayal, and an aggrieved uncle who felt cheated by him. There was nowhere to turn. To appease his brother, the man, Jacob sent his messengers to go ahead of him and ask for Esau's favour. Well, it sounded like the genuine thing to do, except that he had included in his message information about his accumulated wealth through the years. Again, he tried to scheme his way out of a problem he had created.

His strategy failed this time as his messengers said to him upon their return, *"Your brother is coming to meet you, and four hundred men are with him"* (Genesis 32:6b).

Fear gripped him as he fell to his knees in prayer, asking for God's help. Jacob, a man so self-reliant, came to the harsh reality that he was not enough.

What do we do when we have done the best we can, and it's still not enough? Jacob was at this breaking point, and his acquisitions, people, and tactics could not save him. He needed some alone time, perhaps to re-strategize, or rethink. Sending all he had ahead of him, he became his own company.

A stranger soon invaded his private moment. This stranger proved by his actions that this encounter was intentional and purposeful.

"Who does this man think he is?" Jacob thought to himself, puzzled by the stranger's desire to wrestle with him. Jacob clenched tightly, with everything he had. After all, he had always had his way, and this was not going to be an exception.

In the midst of this, he figured, maybe due to the stranger's unflinching determination to not give up the fight, that his opponent was no ordinary person. The feeling was mutual, as the stranger also realized Jacob's strength and unwillingness to yield. How could Jacob relinquish, when this was a struggle to let go of what was for what is to come? His ways for God's ways, and his will in exchange for God's will.

To weaken Jacob, the stranger reached down a little lower and touched his hip joint, thereby dislocating it and reducing his ability to stand firm. *"So Jacob was left alone, and a Man [came and] wrestled with him until daybreak. When the Man saw that He had not prevailed against Jacob, He touched his hip joint; and Jacob's hip was dislocated as he wrestled with Him"* (Genesis 32:24-25 AMP).

In a bid of desperation, powerlessness, and frailty, Jacob clung tightly to this stranger. No longer could he stand straight and tall, for he had lost the ability to support himself.

When the beautiful leaves in our lives become dry and fall away, we are left bare, fragile, and vulnerable. It may be that the job that once paid for our comfortable lifestyle isn't there anymore; or a divorce that arises from a marriage that previously epitomized love, friendship, and intimacy; or a medical diagnosis that steals the spotlight from a previously active and independent life and leaves one dependent on others for daily survival; or the death of a loved one whom we envisioned would be by our side at significant milestones. Like Jacob, we sometimes become incapacitated, unable to let go of the past, understand the present, and move towards the future.

Jacob needed help, but failed to recognize it when it appeared. God had to make Jacob's inadequacy in himself evident. In recognition and acceptance of the limitations of his human nature, Jacob cried out, "*I will not let you go unless you bless me*" (Genesis 32:26b NIV).

He came to the realization that he needed this man, who turned out to be God, for strength for the journey ahead of him; stability to be unmoved and not swayed by life's circumstances; and mobility to get to the place God promised him. That is what God expects of us—not striving with Him, like Jacob first did, but abiding in His love for us and grace available to us. Not trusting in ourselves or our possessions, but putting the weight of our confidence in Him, trusting in what He can empower us to do by His might.

The place where we feel alone is the mid-point between a self-maneuvered past, where we fail to see God lurking in the shadows, and the future, where God is the lead and we are the faithful followers. It is the place our self-dependency ends and God-dependency begins. It is here the old gives way to new beginnings. In this place of aloneness, we also get a name change, from sick to healthy, from debtor to lender, and from ashes to beauty. It is here we experience transformation and begin to see what God sees about us, think His thoughts, and, ultimately, become more like Him.

———————⬤———————

"Write the names of those you believe have ever hurt you and those you have hurt," the voice instructed me. *"We will walk through this together."*

Like Jacob, I'd transitioned from striving with God to abidance. I was willing to trust and obey Him.

"Go through every individual name and pray for each one. Speak blessings over their lives."

"You do not love me," I cried. "Why, oh why, would You ask me to do this?" I was hurt and angry. God's instruction did not seem fair. Boiling hot tears ran down my cheeks.

"This is for your good," said the voice. *"Forgiveness frees you. Let it all go."*

I obeyed, and with each name I struck out on my piece of paper, I felt a massive weight lifted off me and handed over to God. But each strike also took me closer to one name I wanted nothing to do with anymore.

"For the next name, I want you to call her. Tell her you have forgiven her, and pray for her," I thought I heard the voice say.

Or did I? I questioned, in an attempt to disobey this instruction. This was someone I clearly did not want to speak to.

"Yes, you heard me, Osayi."

Adjusting my frame on the couch where I sat, I tearfully gave a detailed narrative of why I never wanted to speak to her again. I slammed the door hard on this instruction and decided I was not going to call her.

"You are disobedient," the voice said in response, and never spoke again.

For two days and nights, I was restless. Wherever I looked, the word "forgive" stared back at me. The word "disobedience" rang continually in my head.

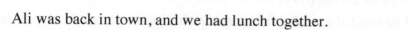

Ali was back in town, and we had lunch together.

"Osayi, whatever you are asked to do, do it. You need to stop fighting God," he advised.

"I will send her a text," I said as a ploy to dismiss the conversation.

But Ali was determined to set me straight as well. "Texting is not calling. Sending an email is not calling. Call her," he said.

For two years, my friend and I had not spoken to each other. Our last conversation was far from amicable. She lashed out words at me that could not be retracted. Oh, I retaliated. With venom in my mouth, I spat out as well. It was a bitter end to what was once a valuable friendship. Now I have to be the one to make this call, when she started it?

I gazed hard and long at my cell phone as I fought within myself the decision to call.

As the phone rang, I hoped that she would not answer. But she did.

"Hey, it's Osayi." And there was silence.

"It's been a while. What's been up with you?" my friend, Cynthia, asked, breaking the silence.

To set the ball of our conversation rolling, I gently told her my reason for calling. Reaching out to her was not as difficult as I thought it would be.

"I fought the decision to speak to you again for two days. Two restless days," I said to my now ex-friend.

"Two days ago?" she asked.

"Yes, two days ago."

"I am glad you did, Osayi. Months after you and I had that big quarrel, I saw you at an event and wanted to come over to ask for your forgiveness. I could not brace myself to do that. Two days ago, I had called a mutual friend requesting your number. I believe God wanted me to call you and do this, but you beat me to it."

Our chat went on longer than I'd expected. We prayed for each other and capped our discussion with words of encouragement.

A burden I had carried for two years suddenly disappeared. Just like that. I felt so light and free.

As I prayed for the people on my list, I could feel the weights of anger, unforgiveness, and even poor self-esteem dropping off and being handed over to God, who had patiently been waiting for me to do this.

"Casting all your cares [all your anxieties, all your worries, and all your concerns, once and for all] on Him, for He cares about you [with deepest affection, and watches over you very carefully]" (1 Peter 5:7 AMP).

It hadn't occurred to me the self-harm I had done by holding people hostage in my heart. By doing so, I'd made myself a prisoner of their actions, decisions, and words. They were not the losers, I was. Now I understood the link between pride and unforgiveness. What others do to us or do not do is not the problem. Who am I not to offer forgiveness to others, especially when I need it myself from God? We must offer to others what we desire to receive from God.

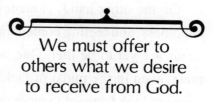

We must offer to others what we desire to receive from God.

"Therefore humble yourselves under the mighty hand of God [set aside self-righteous pride]" (1 Peter 5:6a AMP). It takes humility to face the fact that only God can right every wrong done to us. Only He can vindicate us. We do not have the power to do it ourselves. Attempting to do a job that was meant for the Most High is pride, thinking highly of oneself. No wonder my inability and unwillingness to let go of offenses added more pounds to my spiritual weight.

For the first time, I began to see the beauty in aloneness. Confusing it with loneliness was easy. Aloneness and loneliness, both states of the heart, differ significantly from one another. One who is lonely craves or seeks something external to satisfy an internal craving. The need could be emotional, spiritual, or physical. A lonely person always feels lost in the crowd, empty, unfulfilled, and never satisfied, even when surrounded by loved ones or actively engaged in activities they enjoy. As a result of this dissatisfaction, the lonely person looks externally for what's missing in a bid to fill the void. Unfortunately, it is likened to filling a basket with water. There is no end to it.

On the other hand, aloneness is experiencing beauty, finding happiness, and feeling content in all situations, including when our needs are yet to be met. One who is alone feels whole and complete, even in the midst of lack. It does not mean that the person does not look forward to more or anticipate better, but such desires are not at the cost of their present joy. They have learned not to be defined by anything external, except what lies within them. They see an addition as a complement not a symbol of completion. It is possible to be alone and not experience loneliness.

Still, there are times when aloneness collides with loneliness. We then have a choice to choose the side to which we lean. One could alternate between being alone and being lonely. Our perspective is primarily responsible for what side we find ourselves. Whichever side we settle for influences our emotions, which determine our reactions.

For a long time, I was afraid of being alone, as I found my worth and value in my relationships. I opened myself to people and carried them along, regardless of their opinion or treatment of me. People know when we have made them a god in our lives, and that places us at their mercy. We feel valued and worthy by their affirmations and validations. On the other hand, their rejection reinforces the insignificance and worthlessness we already feel within. We believe they are right about us; therefore, we deserve every ounce of their meanness. Hence, we begin to accept a lie and feel inadequate and unloved. Still, we hold onto them as a drowning person clings to a lifeguard. Eventually, we rip our self-esteem and self-worth to pieces. We cannot find satisfaction in aloneness until we are satisfied in ourselves...until we have found our value, worth, and the definition of who we are.

One morning, I came across a familiar verse in the Bible that says, *"I praise you, for I am fearfully and wonderfully made"* (Psalm 139:14a ESV). Reading that verse made me reflect on my life, again. Did I look or feel like Psalm 139:14? My full name— Osayimwense—is a Nigerian name, and it means "God created me well or wonderfully."

> To find satisfaction in aloneness, we must first be content in ourselves and understand our worth and value.

If I was, then why did I sometimes experience rejection from people I loved?

If I was, then why did I feel so emotionally beat down and hurt?

If I was, then why did I have a trail of failures and mistakes?

Perhaps you have also felt this way, asking questions like "if... then why?" I prayed earnestly about these "ifs" and "whys."

"There are friends I separated you from, some temporarily and others permanently," I heard the voice tell me. *"I need your attention, and some were distractions. Sadly, others your god. Their eyes were your mirror. You saw yourself through their eyes, instead of mine. There are those whose season and assignment in your life are over, and yours is over as well in their lives. Others left because they wanted to. Every challenge you have ever had, every question you have asked, made you seek me, and brought you closer to me. It is all in your perspective."*

I knew God did not cause me pain, for the Bible says that His plans for me are unbelievably and unfathomably good (Jeremiah

29:11), but I do know that He used all of my decisions, actions, inactions, tests, successes, failures, what I did or didn't do, and what others did or didn't do, to get me to this place.

"If I, indeed, was wonderfully made, how come there were times when I did not like myself?" I asked again. No one would believe me if I told them that, but it was true.

"You cannot find satisfaction in aloneness until you are satisfied in yourself. Circumstances and experiences have so defined you to the extent that you no longer see yourself beyond them. The more you focused on people, things or what's happened to you, the more you tarnished your identity and worth.

"You are created in My image and likeness. Look to Me for your identity. Your worth is in Me. You need to settle the issue of your identity, worth, and value in Me; otherwise, you will end up shortchanged in life."

As this voice spoke to me and led me, I read through and meditated on scriptures that affirmed my identity in Christ. The truth in His Word had to sink in. I discovered that God created me in alignment with His Word. I am *everything* His Word says I am. I am complete in Him (Colossians 2:10a AMP). The revelation of that truth made me realize I could not expect people or things to make me whole and worthy. It was never their place, so they could not do a good job at it. I am not saying it's wrong and unbiblical to speak affirming and assuring words to people; our words are to edify, encourage, and strengthen others (Ephesians 4:29). I am saying that no amount of human affirmation can reveal one's identity to them. Validating an individual struggling with identity issues will only produce short-term benefits. Once the effects wane, they will need a refill of that affirmation. Our Maker, God, gives us our identity (Psalm 100:3), and relying on people's affirmation of our identity limits us to the perception and expectation they have of us.

The NIV version of Colossians 2:10a says, *"And in Christ you have been brought to fullness."* Only Christ can reach into the empty wells in our lives and fill them with His love. No one else, no matter how they try, can achieve that task. Our identity needs to be so reliable and stable in Christ that we can still stand tall and unshakable in the absence of our desires. For these desires, be they material possessions, wealth, relationships, or more, though needed, do not define us.

That was the missing link in my life. I needed to know for myself who I was and to whom I belonged. The real work was exchanging the lies I had become accustomed to for the truth. Like concrete, the lies of poor self-esteem, unforgiveness, self-destructive thoughts and habits, had, over time, solidified.

I stood in front of my mirror one day and loudly proclaimed, "I am fearfully and wonderfully made." I needed to believe deep down inside that I am who God says I am. I was created thoughtfully by Him, regardless of what life or circumstances have told me.

Suddenly, I heard a voice speak to me, contradicting what I was saying to myself. The voice reminded me why I was not what God said I was. It brought to my memory painful reasons why I shouldn't believe what God has said. I knew this voice was evil because of how sad and worthless it made me feel about myself. Just when I was about to attend this private pity party, I heard another voice speak to me. It was different, encouraging, liberating, and familiar. It was the voice that had guided me since the start of this journey.

"Keep going. Keep seeing yourself the way I see you. Keep thinking my thoughts towards you. Go into the Word and discover yourself," the voice cheered me on as it brought to mind more scriptures on identity.

I liked this voice better. More still, I liked the person behind the voice. He always affirmed me. I could tell He loved me. He was like my daddy.

There was a time in my life when my soul was hungry for love, affirmation, and attention. I knew I was loved and accepted by my family and friends, but I was having a tough season and needed to confide in someone. I called my dad on the phone and genuinely expressed my feelings and concerns to him.

"Don't ever say that, Osayi," my daddy said. "You mean the world to me, so do not believe that you do not matter. Your coming to this world brought me so much joy. You brighten this family and those who are privileged to know you. Please do not dwell on negative thoughts or allow experiences to dictate to you who you are."

I was high for a long time on those comforting and reassuring words. I wrote them down and saved them. Whenever I felt frustrated, my father's words would ring in my ears again and help me bounce back. But, as I mentioned earlier, the impact of those words gradually faded, and soon I needed another boost. We can never be whole if we constantly feed off human validations and acceptance.

74

This season, wherein I had expected to sink into depression, became a significant and rewarding period of my life. Rather than focus on what was wrong, I turned my gaze in the other direction and took advantage of the blessing in being alone. It was in a moment of self-reflection that God opened my eyes to see the real me. He exposed me to me—my strengths, successes, failures, fears, and shortcomings. Gradually, He took off my false layers of self-reliance and replaced them with steel-coated layers of "Godfidence"—total confidence in God and what He could do in me and through me.

He pulled me into deeper levels of intimacy, and never let me go, even if I wanted. In hindsight, I can see that the journey had never been about others, it was about my God and me. The obedience God could not get from me on the mountain top, I willingly submitted to Him in the valley. God had me to Himself, distraction-free. He used this place to reveal Himself to me, His character and His love for me. I realized that God is highly invested in our ride to destiny, for what we learn along the way matters to Him.

This was my place of transformation. Here, I caught a vision for my future. My identity got established and firmly rooted. I knew who I was. Better still, I knew whose I was. No longer did I have to walk around burdened. No longer did I have to allow the past to dictate my future. I got healed from pain, shame, and everything that tried to make me bow my head in defeat. My confidence sky-rocketed, and I walked with my head held high. All this because of the voice I chose to listen to in this place.

Many voices speak to us in the down moments of our lives. There is one voice that speaks to ensure that we remain trapped in this place. It comes to take our focus away from the lessons we are to learn here, and steal our energy so we do not progress. It attempts to derail us and prevent us from getting to a stronger ending. There is another voice that communicates to us the beauty of this season. It reminds us that the period, though challenging, is not permanent. It sustains us so we can keep hope alive, and strengthens us to go through trials and tests courageously. It speaks to teach us, guide us, comfort us, and lead us out in triumph.

The voice we hearken to in this place determines if we end up with rewards of transformation, progress, healing, and guidance or with regrets by remaining stuck in the perpetuity of blame, frustration, and anger. If you are in the desert seasons of life, are you on the look-out for the blessings in your places and seasons of discomfort? Or are you more captivated by the streams in the wilderness than by the giver of the streams? Are you listening to His voice in the silence of your heart?

As time went on, I began to understand that the voice was beyond a voice. It was indicative of its speaker. So, I chose to dwell more and acknowledge the presence of the speaker. The more I did so, the more I realized that the presence was indeed the game changer for me.

What would I have done without the Person behind the voice? I was gradually standing on my feet because of the One who stayed with me, spoke to me, and guided me to resources to help me understand this season better. I believe this Person is worth knowing, and I bet you think so, too.

Chapter Five

THE GAME CHANGER

"I will never [under any circumstances] desert you [nor give you up nor leave you without support, nor will I in any degree leave you helpless], nor will I forsake or let you down or relax My hold on you [assuredly not]" (Hebrews 13:5 AMP).

GOODBYES HURT; ESPECIALLY from loved ones we are unlikely to see again. We recall every time we spent with them—the good, bad, and sometimes embarrassing moments. That was the case for this group. For years, they did everything together. Within a company of thirteen people was one who brilliantly stood out from the others. Perhaps He was distinguished by the confidence He exuded when He walked, or maybe it was the wisdom found in His words and how He handled issues. Still, it could have been the boldness and bravery He exhibited in fulfilling His purpose. These qualities, and more, endeared many to Him, causing them to move on from all they had ever known into an unknown future, with Him.

After three years of leading the twelve, He began speaking to them about His imminent departure. How could He ever think of leaving them? They had left everything for Him. Some left businesses, habits, relationships, identities, and more, yet He decided to leave them so soon. They must have felt pain, hurt, and loss. This man, Jesus, in only three years was to them and many others a friend (John 15:15), a provider (Matthew 17:27), a leader and a teacher (John 13:13), a protector (John 17:12), a companion (Mark 6:31), a healer (Matthew 8:14-15). Now they wondered what would become of their lives after He left.

Jesus went on speaking, passing instructions on what they needed to do next after His departure. He knew how significant He was to them and the impact His absence would create in their lives. Conscious of their fears and understanding their plight, He reassuringly said to them, *"And I will ask the Father, and He will give you another Helper (Comforter, Advocate, Intercessor—Counselor, Strengthener, Standby), to be with you forever"* (John 14:16 AMP).

On hearing that, the twelve, who were His disciples, peered closer at His mention of another Helper. Their curiosity ignited as they wondered who this new Helper was. Based on what Jesus said to them, this coming Helper was going to be with them *forever*; a sure promise that they would never be alone.

Jesus continued, *"But I tell you the truth, it is to your advantage that I go away; for if I do not go away, the Helper (Comforter, Advocate, Intercessor—Counselor, Strengthener, Standby) will not come to you; but if I go, I will send Him (the Holy Spirit) to you [to be in close fellowship with you]"* (John 16:7 AMP).

When Jesus was on Earth, He was in physical form and so could not be in more than one place at the same time. However, this coming Helper would be with them every step of the way. He would stand by them and be to them what Jesus would have been if He were still present in their midst. No wonder Jesus said to them, *"It is to your advantage that I go away."*

"And He, when He comes, will convict the world about [the guilt of] sin [and the need for a Savior], and about righteousness, and about judgment: about sin [and the true nature of it], because they do not believe in Me [and My message]; about righteousness [personal integrity and godly character], because I am going to My Father and you will no longer see Me; about judgment [the certainty of it], because the ruler of this world (Satan) has been judged and condemned. I have many more things to say to you, but you cannot bear [to hear] them now"* (John 16:8-12 AMP).

> The promise of the Holy Spirit is to ensure we are never alone.

Even Jesus understood the importance of timing in communication. His disciples were not yet ready and mature enough to hear all He had to say to them. They walked with Him but were still clueless about His identity.

There was a time when Jesus desired to feed the multitude that had come a long way to see Him. His disciples, recognizing they had nothing in this deserted place to satisfy the hunger of the multitude—five thousand men, excluding the women and children—advised Jesus to send them away. Rather than heed to their suggested solution, Jesus demanded of them what they could not achieve in their own strength or capacity.

"But He replied, 'You give them something to eat!' And they asked Him, 'Shall we go and buy 200 denarii worth of bread and give it to them to eat?' He said to them, 'How many loaves do you

*have? Go look!' And when they found out, they said, 'Five [loaves],
and two fish'"* (Mark 6:37-38 AMP).

Not only were the multitude miraculously fed by Jesus with
the little supply available, but the leftovers filled twelve baskets.
What happened in the disciples' presence was noteworthy. Such a
large need met by as little as five loaves and two fish. One would
imagine that this supernatural act would be an added feather in
Jesus' cap and increase the disciples' understanding of His identity. Surprisingly, not so.

Soon after, Jesus was in the desert with another multitude—
four thousand men excluding women and children. For three days,
they had had nothing to eat. And Jesus again said, *"'If I send them
away to their homes hungry, they will faint [from exhaustion] on
the road; because some of them have come a long way.' His disciples replied to Him, 'Where will anyone be able to find enough
bread here in this isolated place to feed these people?' He asked
them, 'How many loaves [of bread] do you have?' They said,
'Seven'"* (Mark 8:3-4 AMP).

Having witnessed the groundbreaking miracle of feeding the
five thousand with only five loaves of bread, it remains shocking
that Jesus' disciples wondered where to find food enough for a
lesser crowd. This time, they had more supplies than before. How
could they forget the previous testimony of increase so soon?
We find reasonable explanations for their lack of understanding
here: *"Because they had not understood [the miracle of] the loaves
[how it revealed the power and deity of Jesus]; but [in fact] their
heart was hardened [being oblivious and indifferent to His amazing
works]"* (Mark 6:52 AMP).

Jesus, aware that His disciples were blinded to who He was despite all they had seen Him do, addressed them saying, *"Though you have eyes, do you not see? And though you have ears, do you not hear and listen [to what I have]? And do you not remember, when I broke the five loaves for the five thousand, how many baskets full of broken pieces you picked up?' They answered, 'Twelve.' 'And [when I broke] the seven [loaves] for the four thousand, how many large baskets full of broken pieces did you pick up?' And they answered, 'Seven.' And He was saying to them, 'Do you still not understand?'"* (Mark 8:18-21 AMP).

Aren't we sometimes like these disciples, following whom we do not understand? Serving a God we have head knowledge of, but no heart knowledge of. Like them, we are often blinded to who He is and what it means to be saved by Him or identified with Him. So bad it is that many now attribute the mighty workings of His power to luck, coincidence, or ability. Jesus knew that many of us would not be different from these early disciples. We would identify with Him, yet have no personal knowledge of Him. So He went on in His vivid description of the Helper and His role in the lives of the disciples. He said:

"But when He, the Spirit of Truth, comes, He will guide you into all the truth [full and complete truth]. For He will not speak on His own initiative, but He will speak whatever He hears [from the Father—the message regarding the Son], and He will disclose to you what is to come [in the future]. He will glorify and honour Me, because He (the Holy Spirit) will take from what is Mine and will disclose it to you. All things that the Father has are Mine. Because of this I said that He [the Spirit] will take from what is Mine and will reveal it to you" (John 16:13-15 AMP).

In simple terms, the Holy Spirit would continually reveal Jesus to them—His person, His love, His character, and all that He is. For Jesus to say to the disciples that the Holy Spirit will take information from Him—Jesus—and reveal it to them signifies that the Holy Spirit and Jesus were constantly in communion with one another. He was leaving the Holy Spirit behind for their benefit. We can only reveal things about someone to the level of information we have about them or to the extent that we know them. The Holy Spirit is not an outsider waiting for Jesus to exit the scene so He can jump right in. He was, in fact, with Jesus when He lived on earth as a man. We see Him come upon Jesus in the form of a dove in Luke 3:22. After that encounter, He led Him into the wilderness, where Jesus overcame every temptation the devil brought His way (Luke 4:1).

The Holy Spirit would remove the blinders from the disciples' hearts, eyes, and minds so they could understand Him better. He would lead them to the right word for every circumstance and teach them what they needed to know. The Holy Spirit would also see to it that they did not live in the dark, unaware of what is happening around them, or to them. He would provide them with "insider" information when needed. Jesus never walked ignorantly. He knew what was cooked up against Him by the Pharisees and Sadducees. He knew His betrayer and the one to deny Him later on.

———————◉———————

The weights of fear, doubts, and "what ifs" must have dropped off the disciples' shoulders at Jesus' description of the Holy Spirit. They were no longer skeptical of their future without Jesus. Jesus on earth was God in flesh, and could only be in one place at a time. The Holy Spirit, however, would be with them every time and everywhere, for He did not have the limitations of a human body, like Jesus did while on earth. They certainly did not look forward to Jesus' departure, but they were confident in His promise that they would never be alone. Everything Jesus was to them, the Holy Spirit would be. Not as an imitation, doing what Jesus would do in the same manner He would have done it, but as a replacement to glorify Jesus. The Holy Spirit would also disclose to them God's love for them; the significance of Jesus' death and resurrection; the joy of identifying with Christ; and the power available to them to do all Christ required of them.

Peter, one of the disciples, got a sneak peek of what the Holy Spirit was capable of when Jesus engaged him and others in a conversation. *"Now when Jesus went into the region of Caesarea Philippi, He asked His disciples, 'Who do people say that the Son of Man is?' And they answered, 'Some say John the Baptist; others, Elijah; and still others, Jeremiah, or [just] one of the prophets.' He said to them, 'But who do you say that I am?'"* (Matthew 16:13-15 AMP). It was not a case of flipping the coin to ascertain His identity correctly, and He did not give them options. But *"Simon Peter replied, 'You are the Christ (the Messiah, the Anointed), the Son of the living God.' Then Jesus answered him, 'Blessed [happy, spiritually secure, favored by God] are you, Simon son of Jonah, because flesh and blood (mortal man) did not reveal this to you, but My Father who is in heaven'"* (Matthew 16:16-17 AMP).

Jesus, possibly not wanting Peter to feel superior to the others, quickly let him know that his natural mind, or human wisdom was not the source of this revelation. There was a divine aspect at work here. If one looked at Peter at the time he revealed Jesus as the Son of God, the only people he or she would have seen around Peter were the other disciples. Like Peter, they were all human. How then could the Father not be there and still have access to Peter's mind? It was none other but God's Spirit, the Holy Spirit, who gave Peter that information, for only God's Spirit knows God's thoughts.

"For God has unveiled them and revealed them to us through the [Holy] Spirit; for the Spirit searches all things [diligently], even [sounding and measuring] the [profound] depths of God [the divine counsels and things far beyond human understanding]. For what person knows the thoughts and motives of a man except the man's spirit within him? So also no one knows the thoughts of God except the Spirit of God. Now we have received, not the spirit of the world, but the [Holy] Spirit who is from God, so that we may know and understand the [wonderful] things freely given to us by God" (1 Corinthians 2:10-12 AMP).

"If you, then, being evil [that is, sinful by nature], know how to give good gifts to your children, how much more will your heavenly Father give the Holy Spirit to those who ask and continue to ask Him" (Luke 11:13 AMP).

The gift of the presence of the Holy Spirit to the disciples is as relevant today as it was in biblical times. Anyone who has verbally confessed Jesus as his or her Lord is now His disciple. Shortly before His departure to heaven, Jesus charged His disciples to *"make disciples of all nations"* (Matthew 28: 19). When we win a soul for Jesus Christ, and teach them how to live by faith in Jesus, we are making disciples for Him. To the past, present, and future disciples; the promise, presence, and purpose of the Holy Spirit still holds true today. The Holy Spirit is to us what Jesus was to the early disciples when He lived on earth.

When Jesus was earth as man, He was full of love and compassion. These attributes led Him to attend to the needs of others. He displayed His emotions and understood what it meant to love, to be hurt, and to be betrayed. He built and continually nourished

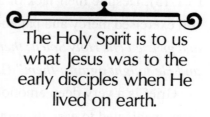

The Holy Spirit is to us what Jesus was to the early disciples when He lived on earth.

His relationships with others. If the Holy Spirit was coming as a replacement, did He understand how to be in touch with us—humans—as Jesus was?

Could He empathize with us as Jesus did with the sick, hungry, and rejected? (John 5: 8)

Could He experience the pain of our rejection and betrayal as Jesus did when betrayed and denied by His own? (Luke 22:48)

Did He have a mind and will of His own as Jesus did when He selected those He walked with and taught? (Matthew 9:8-9; Mark 5:18-20)

Like Jesus, the Holy Spirit has emotions—Emotions are our instinctive reactions or responses to circumstances. They let us know we are human. Israel's stay in the wilderness after God delivered them from the Egyptians was complaint-filled. As a people, they failed to appreciate what God had done, and was doing, for them. They did not remember how He made a way for them through the Red Sea when they were trapped between the Sea and the Egyptians (Exodus 14:15-21). They forgot how He brought out water from the hard rock to quench their thirst (Exodus 17:6-7), and satisfied their hunger by providing them with food (Exodus 16:1-15). Despite their lack of appreciation for these things, God still exercised mercy and patience with them. Until *"they rebelled and grieved His Holy Spirit; therefore He changed into their enemy and He fought against them"* (Isaiah 63:10 AMP).

Grief is a very deep emotion. So sorrowful is it that some are often medicated to ease its pain. God was very patient with Israel until they grieved His Holy Spirit with their repetitious whining and amnesia. In Isaiah 63:10, we see how patient God was with Israel until they caused pain to His Spirit. The journey from their land of captivity to the land of their promise was not easy, but God expected them to always recall the times He had come through for them. A reminder for you and me to never forget what God has done for us when confronted with circumstances that threaten to bring the worst out of us.

Israel was unrepentant, never turning from their disobedience and rebellion. The pain God's Spirit felt triggered His response to their actions. We need to understand the character of the Holy Spirit to know why His being grieved is a problem. The existence of *"love, joy, peace, patience, kindness, goodness, faithfulness, gentleness, and self-control"* (Galatians 5:22-23) in a person, group, or an environment is proof of the Holy Spirit's presence. When He is there, and we choose to act in ways that are contrary to His character and the evidence of His presence, we become at odds with the very thing He represents. That discordance hurts Him.

The Holy Spirit is patient and gentle, so it does take a lot to overwhelm Him to the point of grief. He counsels us multiple times, only for us to do the opposite. He leads us, only to see us head in the other direction. Just as we feel hurt when our loved ones resist or reject our advice or opinion, so the Holy Spirit feels when we undervalue His presence, guidance, and counsel.

In the Bible, many toyed with the gift of His presence through sin, disobedience, and pride. The cost of that was His departure; an absence well felt, for He is indeed a friend that sticks close. King David cried out to God after committing adultery with Bathsheba, *"Do not cast me away from Your presence, And do not take Your Holy Spirit from me"* (Psalm 51:11 AMP). He knew his actions would evoke a sad feeling in this companion who had stood by Him through all the times he was despised, forgotten, and unloved. It could be that he remembered what became of his predecessor, Saul, after the Holy Spirit left him. In the Old Testament, God gave the Holy Spirit to people He assigned or gifted to do a specific task for Him. The Holy Spirit was very vital in the creation of the world in Genesis 1 and in the resurrection of Jesus from the dead in Romans 8:11. *"And if the Spirit of Him who raised Jesus from the dead lives in you, He who raised Christ Jesus from the dead will also give life to your mortal bodies through His Spirit, who lives in you"* (Romans 8: 11 AMP). When Saul was anointed by God to be King of Israel, the prophet Samuel said to him that God's Spirit will come on him and he will now be empowered to do what he had not done before (1 Samuel 10:6). The word was fulfilled in Saul's life in 1 Samuel 10:10. Unfortunately, Saul's disobedience led to the departure of the Holy Spirit (1 Samuel 16: 14). That was the Old Testament. The good news is that Jesus promised in the New Testament that the Holy Spirit will be with us *always*, but we are advised not to grieve (Ephesians 4:30), or quench (1 Thessalonians 5:19) His presence in our lives. *"Do not quench [subdue, or be unresponsive to the working and guidance of] the [Holy] Spirit"* (1 Thessalonians 5: 19 AMP).

If you have ever been harshly criticized, you can attest to the fact that something goes off on inside of you. Maybe you just developed a new skill or learned a new activity, only to have the people dear to your heart rip you, or your new skill, apart. The more you pay attention to the words of the critic, the more your desire to learn and develop fades. Anyone who has felt this way understands what it means to quench the presence of the Holy Spirit. In the New Testament, He does not leave us, but we make His presence of no effect when we unrepentantly sin or disobey God. We are the ones that miss out on a rewarding and exciting relationship with Him if this happens.

Living an ungodly life does not only grieve the Holy Spirit but douses Him over time. The same way we lose interest in what we once loved due to constant criticism and ridicule, the same way He is put off by our consistent and unchanging actions that displease Him. Fanning the flames of His presence requires our obedience to please God, willingness to forgive others, and humility to submit to His leading towards a godly lifestyle.

The Holy Spirit is not associated with only negative emotions. Some of the fruits of the Holy Spirit (Galatians 5:22-23), such as love and joy, are deep, positive emotions expressed by His presence.

Like Jesus, the Holy Spirit has a will—No matter how much God desires us to honour and serve Him, He still gives us the power of choice. *"But if serving the Lord seems undesirable to you, then choose for yourselves this day whom you will serve"* (Joshua 24:15a NIV). As a result of this power, we are held accountable for our decisions. Our will is evidenced by the choices and decisions we make daily.

"Now about the spiritual gifts [the special endowments given by the Holy Spirit], brothers and sisters, I do not want you to be uninformed. Now there are [distinctive] varieties of spiritual gifts [special abilities given by the grace and extraordinary power of the Holy Spirit operating in believers], but it is the same Spirit [who grants them and empowers believers]. All these things [the gifts, the achievements, the abilities, the empowering] are brought about by one and the same [Holy] Spirit, distributing to each one individually just as He chooses" (1 Corinthians 12:1, 4, 11 AMP).

In 1 Corinthians 12, we see that the Holy Spirit has His will. Yes, He hears from the Father and Jesus, and communicates to us, but He is not just an onlooker in our affairs; He has His purpose. Nevertheless, whatever He chooses to do will always align with the will of God the Father and God the Son, for the three of them, though separately distinct, are one (1 Peter 5:7).

The Holy Spirit is the giver of gifts and talents. Not only does He give gifts, but He also empowers us to use those gifts. When God wanted the Israelites to build the tabernacle after they had left Egypt, He pointed out a man called Bezalel from the tribe of Judah and said, *"I have filled him with the Spirit of God in wisdom and skill, in understanding and intelligence, in knowledge, and in all kinds of craftsmanship, to make artistic designs for work in gold, in silver, and in bronze, and in the cutting of stones for settings, and in the carving of wood, to work in all kinds of craftsmanship"* (Exodus 31:3-5 AMP). There were many others within that tribe whom God could have chosen, but He picked Bezalel. The Holy Spirit was going to work with him and enable him in specific areas—wisdom, skill, and all forms of craftsmanship—for this particular mission.

Jesus, at the start of His ministry, testified that the Spirit of God had come upon Him and anointed Him to preach, heal, and deliver the captives (Luke 4:18 KJV). Another word for anointing is "empowerment." Jesus' calling preceded His birth, but the empowerment of the Holy Spirit revealed His gifts and calling. At Jesus' baptism, where the Holy Spirit came upon Him, many others were getting baptized. Still, the Holy Spirit exercised His will, in conformity to God the Father, and rested on Jesus. After Jesus had departed, His disciples were worshipping together when the Holy Spirit selected from their midst Barnabas and Saul for the assignment He had for them (Acts 13:2). Like Jesus, who freely chose His relationships and willfully died on the cross for us, the Holy Spirit has a will.

Like Jesus, the Holy Spirit has a voice—We express our voice in many ways, including writing, singing, painting, and drawing. Through these channels, we tell our stories, give life to our feelings, emphasize a point and even make decisions. Jesus told His disciples that the Holy Spirit would teach, guide, and even say things to them that would happen in the future. This means that He could communicate with them.

Adam and Eve had just committed the very act God had warned them against—eating from the tree of the knowledge of good and evil. While attempting to cover their nakedness, having been exposed by their act of disobedience, they heard the voice of God and hid. Genesis 3:8-10 in the King James Version says, *"And they heard the voice of the Lord God walking in the garden in the cool of the day: and Adam and his wife hid themselves from the presence of the*

Lord God amongst the tress of the garden. And the Lord God called unto Adam, and said unto him, Where art thou? And he said, I heard thy voice in the garden, and I was afraid, because I was naked; and I hid myself." They hid from His voice because it signified something more profound—the presence of its speaker. It was obvious they had a relationship with God. We hear someone's voice loudly or faintly depending on our proximity to the speaker.

Adam did not appear frightened that God walked in the garden to meet with him. His recognition of God's voice revealed how often they interacted. Only this time, his response was like that of a child caught with his hand in a cookie jar. God's walk in the garden to connect with Adam is similar to the way Jesus walked with and related to His

> We hear someone's voice loudly or faintly depending on our proximity to the speaker.

disciples while He was on earth. The promise of the Holy Spirit by Jesus is to ensure that, like Adam and the disciples, we also have a personal and intimate relationship with God. With the Holy Spirit, we will never walk alone, or be alone.

The more time we spend with the Holy Spirit, the more we recognize His voice amidst others. The Holy Spirit cares. He wants intimacy. He wants to speak to me and to you, just like Jesus did before He departed earth. His emotions, His will, and His voice let us know that the Holy Spirit has a personality and can connect with us on an individual level, like Jesus did with the disciples, and God with Adam and Eve.

Though unseen in a physical form, the Holy Spirit knows what it's like to feel, to have His will, and communicate with us.

91

Chapter Six

HIS VOICE

"And after the earthquake a fire; but the Lord was
not in the fire: and after the fire a still small voice"
(1 Kings 19:12 KJV).

ELIJAH WAS A man of courage. In the presence of the king, he declared a season of drought over the land, which came to pass. His next public appearance was to challenge the prophets of Baal to a contest, openly, to prove that the Lord is God alone. After a victorious display of God's power, demonstrated by God's acceptance of the sacrifice Baal could not receive, and the outpouring of rain, bringing an end to the drought, Elijah's popularity soared. But only for a moment. A death threat from the king's wife, Jezebel, sent Elijah's world crashing down. In a flash, he went from being victorious to being a fugitive, finding safety in the wilderness. Little did he know that his weary emotional, spiritual, and mental state was an invitation for God's visitation.

Don't get me wrong, a wilderness experience is not the recipe to have an intimate encounter with God or to experience Him. But many of us are so occupied with activities that we rarely pull up a chair, sit, and spend time with God until life brings us to a halt. We are more focused on *doing* for Him than *being* with Him. "Just like Elijah, whose response to God in the following verse testified of his busyness. *"He said, 'I have been very zealous (impassioned) for the Lord God of hosts (armies) [proclaiming what is rightfully and uniquely His]; for the sons of Israel have abandoned (broken) Your covenant, torn down Your altars, and killed Your prophets with the sword. And I, only I, am left; and they seek to take away my life'"* (1 Kings 19:10 AMP).

Elijah was a prophet that fearlessly spoke God's truth at all times to the Israelites. He had an intimate relationship with God, evidenced by his ability to hear God's instructions per time. After Elijah predicted a three-year drought in the land of Israel, God spoke to him, redirecting him to the brook Cherith where there were provisions for his sustenance. His relationship with God exempted him from the calamity that had befallen others as a result of the drought. When the supplies ran out, God spoke to him about the location for his next provision.

> We need to change direction and focus more on being with God than doing for God. It does not mean that doing for God is not important, but the strength for that doing flows from our being with Him.

When the drought neared its end, God communicated to Elijah the next steps to take for the release of rain in Israel. He said to him, *"Go, show yourself to Ahab, and I will send rain on the face of the earth"* (1 Kings 18: 1b AMP). Elijah showed himself to Ahab as God commanded him to and it was in that meeting, Elijah demanded the contest between Baal and God. We do not know the exact point Elijah became weary, but we know he was, for after he ran away from Jezebel into the wilderness, he said, *"It is enough; now, O Lord, take my life, for I am no better than my fathers"* (1 Kings 19: 4 AMP).

The Bible makes it clear in Isaiah 30:15 that we gain strength from quietness; not necessarily physical stillness but spiritual stillness. In quietness, we free ourselves from fear, doubt, unforgiveness, and bitterness. Our spirit becomes open to hearing what He has to say to us, even in the hard seasons of life. In quietness and stillness, the transmission between our spirit and God's Spirit is unhindered.

God did come to speak to Elijah, but not in the dramatic way Elijah expected. The wind came, but God was not in it, though God had spoken in times past through this medium to a man called Job (Job 38:1). Surely, Elijah must have thought, when he saw the earthquake, that God was in it as well, but He was not. And then the fire came. God had spoken to the Israelites while in the wilderness from the fire (Deuteronomy 5:24), but this time, the fire was void of His presence. Suddenly, Elijah's environment became quiet, and he heard a still, small voice dropping nuggets of information in his mind as God's Spirit interacted with his spirit. Just as humans speak in different ways, so does the Holy Spirit. One way in which He speaks is with the still, small voice, as seen in the case of Elijah.

The Holy Spirit lives inside of us. Even though He has a personality, He is a Spirit like us. Humans are spirits living in a body; hence, the Holy Spirit speaks to our spirit. Man was nothing when formed, until God breathed into Him the breath of life. That breath was God transmitting His Spirit into man, and man became a living being (Genesis 2: 7). After His resurrection from the dead, but before His ascension to heaven, Jesus also breathed on His disciples. As He did so, He said to them in John 20:22, *"Receive the Holy Spirit."* Jesus gave them what He had. Throughout His ministry, Jesus was not alone.

As our breath is unseen yet its impact undeniable, so it is with the Holy Spirit. His presence is as close as our breath; invisible with an invaluable impact. To hear the still, small voice requires us to be intentionally still and at rest in our spirit. Quiet. We need to remove the clutter, letting go of our worries, fears, anger, and anything that overwhelms us. As we free our mind of these, we allow the transmission of infor-

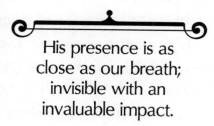

His presence is as close as our breath; invisible with an invaluable impact.

mation between the Holy Spirit and our spirit. The Bible says in 1 Corinthians 2:16 that we *"have the mind of Christ."* The mind of Christ is no ordinary mind. It is one that is renewed and unwilling to give room to the weights, cares, and worries of the world. That is the mind that discerns the conversation our spirit has with the Holy Spirit.

Early in this season of my life, I had an experience with the presence of the Holy Spirit, evidenced by the still, small voice. It gave me reverential fear that God sees everything I do. Everything. Summer had just begun, and in a city where we had more cold days than hot, I wanted to get out as often as I could. I was not at the right place emotionally for anything fun, but I knew

I'd be hurting myself more if I failed to make the most of this brief summer season.

Now, I was involved in the church God had led me to months ago. My much-anticipated summer season was now the season of evangelism in the church. Members were expected to meet up every Saturday, pray together, and head out in small groups to minister to people in the community. Like I said, I did not feel like I was at the right place to minister to anyone. If anything, I needed to be ministered to. Confusion about everything that happened and the speed of its occurrence beclouded my mind and emotions.

When I finally garnered strength, I drove to the church building, only to meet an empty hall. Everyone had gathered, prayed, and already left in small groups. Outwardly, I appeared disappointed and upset with myself for not sticking to schedule and for allowing my emotions to string me along. However, deep down, I excitedly thought to myself, "At least God knows I tried." I picked up my phone to call a member of the church to know how far gone they were. My aim was to inform her of my failed attempt to be a part of the gathering, so I could get a pass for the little effort I made in showing up.

Interestingly, she was not far from the church premises and asked me to meet her to collect some outreach materials. After collecting the materials, I got in my car and instead of conducting the outreach, drove home. I had barely walked through my doors at home when a voice within me spoke. It was discernible. I could have mistaken it for just random thoughts, except its message was very precise.

"Osayi, now that you are home, I want you to go and evangelize to the people in your neighbourhood."

"What people?" I asked in my spirit. At that time, my knowledge about the person of the Holy Spirit was just developing, so I was still a bit unsure of what was happening. However, I was spiritually alert enough to pick up the dialogue.

As I prepared myself to head out again, I heard Him say to me, *"Go with sixty dollars, Osayi."*

This time, I paused and reasoned aloud, "Why do I need money to distribute these gospel outreach materials on the street?" Seeing that it made no sense to me, I stepped out of my house without my wallet.

Walking past the convenience store a block away from my building, I heard the voice say to me, *"Turn left and keep going."*

I was not so sure if that was the Holy Spirit, but I made the turn. Approaching a group of people who appeared homeless, the Holy Spirit pointed out a couple and said, *"Osayi, those two individuals over there need that money. You still have time. Why don't you go home and get your card to withdraw cash at the convenience store?"*

Minutes later, I arrived where the group stood and began handing out the outreach materials to them. They all walked away from me, rejected the materials and crossed to the other side of the road. All, except these two individuals.

"What is that in your hands?" the lady, one of the two, asked curiously.

"Oh, it's information about Jesus," I replied, with a lack of confidence stemming from the outright rejection by the others.

Still, I stretched the material further in their direction. That was when her husband, as I later discovered he was, spoke furiously.

"We don't want to hear anything about Jesus or God or any of that," he said, visibly angry. "Here is my wife's prescription for some medication she needs," he added, unfolding a piece of paper he just pulled from his back pocket.

"The government covers a portion of the fee, and all I need is fifty dollars to make it up so she can have the medication. We prayed and told God if He was real, He should send us the money as we have no other way to get it. Instead, what do we get?"

As he spoke, the Holy Spirit said to me, *"Can you see why I wanted you to make the cash withdrawal of sixty dollars?"*

I stood there, frozen at the precision of His direction and guidance. I pleaded with the man and his wife to wait for me, and I quickly dashed home to get my wallet.

Making a quick stop at the closest convenience store, I made a withdrawal and hurried to the same spot, where the couple waited patiently for me. I gave them the money, and the husband pulled his wife close and, with tears in his eyes, said to her, "I told you God places angels in our midst daily. We have met one."

I chatted briefly with them, prayed for them, and finally handed out the prayer pamphlet to them, again. This time, it was accepted.

That evening, as I prepared to sleep, I recalled times when I have heard that still, small voice within and ignored it. Only to realize later how right it was.

"The Spirit himself bears witness with our spirit that we are children of God" (Romans 8:16 ESV).

The witness of the Holy Spirit is another way God confirms His presence in our lives and speaks to us. A person who is not connected to God is likely not going to experience the beauty of the inward witness of the Holy Spirit. It is an assurance that we are God's children. I like the way the Amplified version puts it— *"The Spirit Himself testifies and confirms together with our spirit [assuring us] that we [believers] are children of God"* (Romans 8:16).

The *Merriam Webster's Dictionary* defines the word testify as "to show that something is true or real; to give proof of something."[1] In other words, when we testify of an event or circumstance, we give substance to what we believe to be the truth or the fact. When the Holy Spirit confirms with our spirit, He lays an impression on our heart. We are intuited to positive or negative events, before they happen so we can prepare and position ourselves properly. These impressions prompt us to take certain actions and steps, but also leave us with a decision to make. Do we come in agreement with what is impressed in our spirit by the Holy Spirit? Or do we completely ignore it?

To illustrate this point, think about when a cell phone rings. The moment we answer the call, it stops ringing, and the environment becomes quiet, again. That is what happens when we understand and agree with what the Holy Spirit is saying to us. We become at ease.

However, failing to respond to the phone call allows it to go on ringing, striving to get our attention. Likewise, the Holy Spirit keeps calling out for us when our spirit and His are not in alignment. Disregarding this divine signal creates a tugging and discomfort in our spirit. That pull signifies that He is not in sync with our next move, regardless of what it may be. It could be a relationship, a trip, a decision, a conversation, or even an opportunity. Sometimes, these circumstances may be right, but the timing is wrong. He could be asking us to wait. It is important that we stay awake spiritually and stay close to God when He places anything in our spirit. Only He can provide clarity as to why.

Following the guidance of the Holy Spirit offers us a life void of regrets. The repercussion of disobeying or not hearkening to the witness of the Holy Spirit is devastating. It could be a matter of recognizing and seizing opportunities or missing them altogether. The story of the Shunammite woman in the Bible illustrates how a person can be divinely prompted to identify and seize opportunities. We are unaware of how many times Elisha stopped by her house based on her invitation, but we know that it was more than once. Her hospitality led her to open her doors to him and feed him whenever he passed by her house.

"Now there came a day when Elisha went over to Shunem, where there was a prominent and influential woman, and she persuaded him to eat a meal. Afterward, whenever he passed by, he stopped there for a meal. She said to her husband, 'Behold, I sense that this is a holy man of God who frequently passes our way'" (2 Kings 4:8-9 AMP).

Here was a man with the anointing of God to give her a change of story, yet she had no clue who he was. That was until she perceived his true identity. I believe it was the Spirit of God with her that provided the information. It was necessary so she would improve on how she treated him, as she did in the next verse of the text. *"Please, let us make a small, fully-walled upper room [on the housetop] and put a bed there for him, with a table, a chair, and a lampstand. Then whenever he comes to visit us, he can turn in there"* (2 Kings 4:10 AMP). Her warm reception towards Elisha became the key that unlocked her testimony. She gave birth to her son miraculously, according to Elisha's prophecy.

Not hearkening to what the Holy Spirit has to say through these perceptions or the inward witness could also be a matter of life and death. I learned that the hard way. Having spent the previous day indoors because of a cold, I was eager to get out of bed, dress, and show up for my scheduled appointments. I felt much better that morning than I did the previous day. My cold symptoms had waned overnight, sparing me the embarrassment of blowing my nose and coughing out loud in public.

Barely had I made it out of the bathroom when the symptoms resurfaced. But I had my mind set on leaving the house, and this cold was not going to disrupt my plans. As I stood facing my front door, ready to begin the day, I felt strongly in my spirit that I should stay indoors all day, again. In spite of that, I stepped out. I walked home that evening with a spring in my step. Everything on my itinerary had a check mark next to it. A few blocks from my house, I stepped off the sidewalk onto the street in an attempt to cross to the other side. It was a two-way stop, and the cars had come to a halt. No sooner had I stepped onto the road than the truck to my left turned right. I heard the screeching of the tires...I felt the powerful impact of the vehicle as it hit me on the left side of my body.

Miraculously, I did not fall to the right and onto the ground. Instead, I fell forward. I stood still and in shock, trying to decipher what had just happened. I was soon to find out.

"I am so sorry I hit you. I did not even see you," said the driver, looking terrified, perhaps thinking of the consequences of his action.

"What?" I asked him, in utter disbelief.

"I did not see you standing on the sidewalk. Neither did I see you crossing the street. I did not even know I hit you until you fell."

The sudden realization of how blessed I was to still be on this side of eternity hit home. If I had fallen in the opposite direction of the truck's impact, he would have run me over before knowing I was there. I knew God had pushed me to safety, allowing me to be seen by the driver to avoid more impact. Years ago, I lost an aunt — who was in her twenties at the time — in a car accident, and I saw how devastated my parents were. I was overwhelmed with gratitude to God for sparing my parents a repetition of that agony.

Physical examination by the paramedics minutes later, and diagnostic exams by the doctor the following morning, showed I had no broken bones, no internal bleeding, and no bruises. As I sat in bed at home that evening, the slight pain on my left arm reminded me of my disobedience. *"As it is said, 'Today, if you hear his voice, do not harden your hearts as in the rebellion'"* (Hebrews 3:15 ESV). The slight pain was also a reminder of His mercy and His presence to protect His children. Psalm 91:4 tells us that God covers us with His feathers. That presence and covering is the reason the consequence did not equal the force of the vehicular impact.

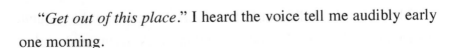

"Get out of this place." I heard the voice tell me audibly early one morning.

Frightened, but overcome with curiosity, I quickly walked to my bedroom door and opened it to see who was there. No one. The realization that I was the only person awake in the apartment I shared with a roommate almost made me jump out of my skin.

I'd moved to a new city temporarily for work. Knowing my duration there was short, I opted for an affordable, comfortable, and non-contractual accommodation.

Later that day, I brought up this experience with my coworker, Cindy, over our dinner date. She was the first person I took a liking to on my first day on this job. From the conversations we'd had so far, I knew she was a Christian with deep spiritual insight.

"I think that was God speaking to you, Osayi," she said, after listening to me.

Not convinced, I went on describing how clear and authoritative the voice was.

"How could that be God? I have no issues where I currently reside. Why would He ask me to leave?" I asked her again.

But as I matured and kept on nurturing my relationship with the Holy Spirit, I understood that the voice I heard came from within my spirit. It is so clearly audible that one can easily assume they heard it with their physical ears. The voice is loud enough for the recipient not to miss its message, even if they tried. The audible voice of the Holy Spirit is one of the ways God speaks to His children. Many times when we hear the voice of the Holy Spirit in this manner, it could be to alert us of dangers just around the corner, prepare us for what is to come, or provide guidance. Having said that, the Holy Spirit reserves the right to choose His means of communication with us, in line with the Scriptures. It is not our place to tell Him how to speak to us.

In no time, Cindy and I found an alternate accommodation for me. I did not understand why I had to make that move, or how to start the conversation with my landlord. But I did not have to worry for long. Days later, I got a call from the apartment owner. An urgent situation had come up with his family and, apologetically, he needed one of the bedrooms to become available in the apartment. Seeing that I was the last person to rent and had only been there for a short period, compared to my roommate, it made sense that I was the one asked to make a move. Our tenancy agreement was fluid enough to allow this, without penalties on either side. He kindly refunded that month's rent and offered me adequate time to find another place.

Then it dawned on me why God had spoken to me, prompting another apartment search. One may wonder why God had to talk to me about something that may seem trivial to some folks, but God knows us more than we know ourselves. He knew us even before we were born (Jeremiah 1:5) and knows how differently we respond to unforeseen challenges. Though there are times when I act maturely in the face of trials and get applauded by those around me, there are also cases where I just cry and complain to anyone who cares to listen about how confused and devastated I am. If God shows concern for the number of hairs on my head, why would He not care about the issues or challenges in my life? Why would He not care about our pain, job loss, relationship struggles, and health challenges? We need to understand that God loves us so much and is interested and invested in every detail of our lives. Luke 12: 7 says, *"Indeed, the very hairs of your head are all numbered. Do not fear; you are more valuable than many sparrows"* (NASB).

> If God shows concern for the number of hairs on my head, why would He not care about the issues or challenges in my life?

Because of the clear voice of the Holy Spirit, I was not panic-stricken, but prepared. I had another accommodation long before I knew why I needed it.

In Acts 10, the Holy Spirit spoke audibly to Peter, informing him of the imminent arrival of Cornelius's messengers. At that time, the Jews and Gentiles rarely associated with one another. None of the Gentiles had been privileged to hear the Gospel. God's next assignment for Peter was not only pioneering but was going to break the barriers that existed between the Jews and Gentiles. With His voice, the Holy Spirit authenticated the instructions and gave Peter the assurance that God wanted him to do this. I doubt Peter would have followed these messengers if he was not convinced, beyond reasonable doubt, that this was the Holy Spirit speaking to him.

"A voice came to him, 'Get up, Peter, kill and eat!' But Peter said, 'Not at all, Lord, for I have never eaten anything that is common (unholy) and [ceremonially] unclean.' And the voice came to him a second time, 'What God has cleansed and pronounced clean, no longer consider common (unholy).' This happened three times, and then immediately the object was taken up into heaven. Now Peter was still perplexed and completely at a loss as to what his vision could mean when the men who had been sent by Cornelius, having asked directions to Simon's house, arrived at the gate. And they called out to ask whether Simon, who was also called Peter, was staying there. While Peter was thoughtfully considering the vision, the Spirit said to him, 'Now listen, three men are looking for you. Get up, go downstairs and go with them without hesitating or doubting, because I have sent them Myself'" (Acts 10:13-20 AMP).

The day the truck hit me, the Holy Spirit had communicated with me through the witness of His Spirit. I had an inkling to remain indoors, even when I did not know why. He could have passed this message across clearly and distinctly, but He did not. We need to know that even in dire situations, the Holy Spirit reserves the right to choose his channel of communication with us. We only need to be more sensitive to His presence and instructions per time.

Chapter Seven

HOW DO I KNOW IT'S YOU, LORD?

"Now the serpent was more crafty than any other
beast of the field that the Lord God had made. He said
to the woman, "Did God actually say, 'You shall not
eat of any tree in the garden?'" (Genesis 3:1 ESV)

IT IS FASCINATING that right after creation the Bible intro-
duces us, almost immediately, to the person behind the fall of man-
kind—Satan. His strategy was covert, and Eve, unable to discern
the intent and impact of the conversation she was having with the
serpent that Satan was speaking through, fell cheaply for his deception. And all Satan used was his voice. God speaks to us. We talk to
ourselves. The devil also speaks, communicating with us through
many channels, as God does.

We need to be able to discern God's voice amidst the others
blasting in our ears. A voice that persuasively or forcefully nudges
us to do the opposite of what God expects of us is clearly not God's
voice. It could be our voice wanting to satisfy our desires in our
own way. It could be the devil wanting us trapped with the guilt of

disobedience to God. It could be others—family, friends, or even the media—who perhaps mean well, but don't know better.

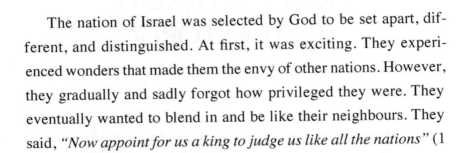

The nation of Israel was selected by God to be set apart, different, and distinguished. At first, it was exciting. They experienced wonders that made them the envy of other nations. However, they gradually and sadly forgot how privileged they were. They eventually wanted to blend in and be like their neighbours. They said, *"Now appoint for us a king to judge us like all the nations"* (1 Samuel 8:5b ESV). Israel cried out to Samuel, the prophet. Prophets were the medium between God and man. So, Samuel brought their request before God, in prayer. What happened next is a reminder of how God talked to Moses and Abraham, as one does with a friend.

"And the Lord said to Samuel, 'Obey the voice of the people in all that they say to you, for they have not rejected you, but they have rejected me from being king over them. According to all the deeds that they have done, from the day I brought them up out of Egypt even to this day, forsaking me and serving other gods, so they are also doing to you. Now then, obey their voice; only you shall solemnly warn them and show them the ways of the king who shall reign over them'" (1 Samuel 8:7-9 ESV).

Here was the Almighty God, the Immortal, exposing His thoughts to a mortal, a person like you and me. He expressed the rejection He felt from His own and then empathized with how their behaviour affected Samuel. But it wasn't always this way with Samuel and God.

———————◉———————

"Samuel," he heard the voice of his boss, Eli, calling. Hurriedly, he got out of bed with eyes still full of sleep and ran into Eli's room. This scenario happened three times before Eli recognized it was God calling Samuel.

"Then the Lord called Samuel, and he said, 'Here I am!' and ran to Eli and said, 'Here I am, for you called me.' But he said, 'I did not call; lie down again.' So he went and lay down. And the Lord called again, 'Samuel!' and Samuel arose and went to Eli and said, 'Here I am, for you called me.' But he said, 'I did not call, my son; lie down again.' Now Samuel did not yet know the Lord, and the word of the Lord had not yet been revealed to him. And the Lord called Samuel again the third time. And he arose and went to Eli and said, 'Here I am, for you called me.' Then Eli perceived that the Lord was calling the boy. Therefore Eli said to Samuel, 'Go, lie down, and if he calls you, you shall say, 'Speak, Lord, for your servant hears.'' So Samuel went and lay down in his place" (1 Samuel 3:4-9 ESV).

I believe Samuel heard his name audibly being called by God. How did Samuel, who had been serving the Lord in the temple since he was a little boy (1 Samuel 2:22; 1 Samuel 3:1), not recognize the voice of the One whom he had been serving? Thankfully, Eli was there to figure it out for him, or else Samuel would have delayed answering the call, or worse, missed it. Like Samuel, many of us are busy "doing" for a God we do not know personally. I was once like that. For a long time, I sat in the pews of the church, served God and the people, and still did not know God for myself, nor did I believe I could have an intimate relationship with Him.

109

I have met Christians who do not think or believe God wants to communicate with them, so they look to others to be their spiritual bridge to God.

━━━━━━◆━━━━━━

In the Old Testament, prophets were the link between God and the people, and vice versa. Moses, Isaiah, Samuel, Deborah, Jeremiah, and Elijah are examples of prophets whom God used to reach the people. They spoke God's mind and acted on His behalf. That was before the arrival of Jesus. Jesus came for many reasons, primarily to give us eternal life through salvation. The next two verses attest to the reason for coming. *"For God so loved the world, that he gave his only Son, that whoever believes in him should not perish but have eternal life. For God did not send his Son into the world to condemn the world, but in order that the world might be saved through him"* (John 3:16-17 ESV). *"The thief comes only in order to steal and kill and destroy. I came that they may have and enjoy life, and have it in abundance [to the full, till it over-flows]"* (John 10:10 AMP).

The "I" in John 10: 10 above refers to Jesus. Jesus also came to take our place through the exchange on the cross. He died so we might live. He was wounded so we could find our healing (Isaiah 53). He suffered the consequences of our sins so that, through faith in Him, we could be reconciled to God and made right with Him (Romans 3:21-25). Jesus also became poor to make us rich (2 Corinthians 8:9).

When Jesus lived, He showed us how to relate personally to God. He kept calling God His Father, and this direct and personal connection did not sit well with the religious leaders. The moment Jesus gave up His spirit on the cross, the veil of the temple was torn from the top to the bottom, giving everyone unhindered access to God (Matthew 27:51). No longer is access to God only available to a select few, but it is now available to everyone who believes in Jesus Christ (Hebrews 4:16). It does not mean that spiritual leaders, such as prophets, are no longer needed. However, their roles have significantly changed because of what Jesus did. God appoints and anoints them to many offices to lead us to spiritual maturity, so we do not become adults permanently latched onto the breasts of our leaders.

"And [His gifts to the church were varied and] He Himself appointed some as apostles [special messengers, representatives], some as prophets [who speak a new message from God to the people], some as evangelists [who spread the good news of salvation], and some as pastors and teachers [to shepherd and guide and instruct], [and He did this] to fully equip and perfect the saints (God's people) for works of service, to build up the body of Christ [the church]; until we all reach oneness in the faith and in the knowledge of the Son of God, [growing spiritually] to become a mature believer, reaching to the measure of the fullness of Christ [manifesting His spiritual completeness and exercising our spiritual gifts in unity]. So that we are no longer children [spiritually immature], tossed back and forth [like ships on a stormy sea] and carried about by every wind of [shifting] doctrine, by the cunning and trickery of [unscrupulous] men, by the deceitful scheming of people ready to do anything [for personal profit]" (Ephesians 4:11-14 AMP).

We are never mature enough to not need the church for fellowship and the guidance of our spiritual leaders. With the increasing deception in the world today, we cannot do without a Bible-believing church and our leaders. But we shouldn't stay as babies, dependent solely on our leaders to be the middlemen and conduits through which we approach God. *"For there is one God, and there is one mediator between God and men, the man Christ Jesus"* (1 Timothy 2:5 ESV). *"Long ago, at many times and in many ways, God spoke to our fathers by the prophets, but in these last days he has spoken to us by his Son, whom he appointed the heir of all things, through whom also he created the world"* (Hebrews 1:1-2 ESV).

Our leaders access God through Jesus, and we can access God through Jesus as well. This is not a reason for us to stop attending services in the church or listening to our spiritual leaders, for the church is made for fellowship with other Christians; and our church leaders are there to teach, guide, encourage, and support us in our walk with God. They are not there to be our "God" but to point us to Him and help us build and maintain our relationship with God.

> The ability to recognize God's voice is dependent on our understanding of God and His word.

To know our mediator, Jesus, we need to know the Bible. Knowing is a pathway to relationship. The Bible is a complete revelation of who He is. There is no better way to be acquainted with God than to spend time reading the Bible—the Word of God. Not reading it like a textbook, seeking for what makes sense or what is politically correct or incorrect, but reading deliberately and purposefully to meet its author. The Bible is not just a book with principles, as some call it; nor is it a historical document or a collection of interesting stories. The Holy Bible is Jesus Himself written in words. John 1:1 tells us that the Word is God. *"In the beginning was the Word, and the Word was with God, and the Word was God* (John 1: 1 ESV).

———————◆———————

The Trinity—God the Father, God the Son, and God the Holy Spirit—refers to the three persons in the Godhead. God the Son is Jesus Christ, and God the Spirit is the Holy Spirit. They work interdependently, sometimes independently, yet in perfect harmony with one another. All three were present and involved in creation. Genesis 1:1-2 says, *"In the beginning, God created the heavens and the earth. The earth was without form and void, and darkness was over the face of the deep. And the Spirit of God was hovering over the face of the waters"* (ESV). In these verses, we see the presence of God the Father— *"God created the heavens and the earth"*—and God the Holy Spirit—*"The Spirit of God was hovering over the face of the waters."* The following verse begins with, *"And God said"*—continuing all through this chapter of creation— *"And God said, 'Let there be light,' and there was light"* (Genesis 1:3 ESV).

Whenever God spoke during creation, He spoke the Word. In the New Testament, John tells us that, *"In the beginning was the Word, and the Word was with God, and the Word was God. He was in the beginning with God. All things were made through him, and without him was not anything made that was made. And the Word became flesh and dwelt among us, and we have seen his glory, glory as of the only Son from the Father, full of grace and truth"* (John 1:1-3, 14 ESV). We know from these verses that the Word was present at the beginning, the Word was with God, and the Word was also called God. There was nothing that came into existence without the Word. We also see in these verses that Jesus is the Word for He is the only person of the Godhead that was made flesh—became a physical man—and lived among people, as a human being. Whenever God spoke, the words were not ordinary, but full of life, because it was God the Son—Jesus Christ—that was spoken.

However, the Word became known to man and compiled as the Bible by the inspiration of the Holy Spirit. *"And we have the prophetic word more fully confirmed, to which you will do well to pay attention as to a lamp shining in a dark place, until the day dawns and the morning star rises in your hearts, knowing this first of all, that no prophecy of Scripture comes from someone's own interpretation. For no prophecy was ever produced by the will of man, but men spoke from God as they were carried along by the Holy Spirit"* (2 Peter 1:19-21 ESV).

We would not have the Word if the Holy Spirit was not involved. It took all three of them to get us the Bible. You see why fellowship is important. By spending time in the Word, we get to know God—His person, His personality, His character, His plans, and His purposes. We can never discern the voice of the Holy Spirit if we do not know God through the lens of the Scriptures—the Bible.

———————◉———————

The Holy Spirit guides and speaks to us through many channels—directly through the Scriptures, through people, through circumstances or events, through dreams and visions, and through prophecies. However, we need to check these directions against the truths outlined in the Bible. *"Do not quench [subdue, or be unresponsive to the working and guidance of] the [Holy] Spirit. Do not scorn or reject gifts of prophecy or prophecies [spoken revelations—words of instruction or exhortation or warning]. But test all things carefully [so you can recognize what is good]. Hold firmly to that which is good"* (1 Thessalonians 5:19-21 AMP).

The Word Test

One of the litmus tests for His guidance is the Word of God—the Holy Bible. Does what you hear match what the Bible says on the subject matter? The Bible is one of our biggest assets when going through the wilderness seasons of life. Until we know the Word, we can't discern His voice amidst the voices grappling for our attention. From the Word, we become aware of God's ways and His character. The Holy Spirit desires to comfort, strengthen, protect, guide, teach, and help us in the down seasons of life. He wants to be intimate with us and lead us out of the desert. But how can He, if we don't recognize when He guides us?

The Holy Spirit never tells us anything contrary to the Word of God. As we read the Word, the Holy Spirit takes it and reveals to us how it applies to our situation. He may speak to us on things not explicitly stated in the Bible, but they will never contradict the principles that govern the topic of interest in the Bible. Psalm 119:105 says, *"Your word is a lamp for my feet, a light on my path"* (NIV).

My path began crossing with others and I began to build new relationships in the city I lived in, which is Regina. Some old relationships were rekindled amicably. God had made me understand that He needed my attention in this season, and had to separate me from my most powerful distraction—people. But God knows that relationships are very vital to our sustenance and growth, so He does not leave us separated from others beyond our ability to handle the separation. I believe this ability is unique to each person based on our personality, and our emotional and spiritual maturity. I remember praying about many of the new relationships and asking for His thoughts on every one of them. God did not do that for me. God has directly told me about associations in the past. He knew I would make mistakes or take actions in them that would not only hurt me but end up not glorifying Him. But this time around, He wanted me to make the decision for myself, and rather than be direct, He used principles in the Bible to guide my decision in this area.

I was reading the first chapter of Jonah, when God impressed some things on my heart about relationships. *"Do you see how much these sailors lost? No doubt they survived the turbulence, but they lost valuables and properties as they threw them in the water to lighten the ship. That is how much the wrong partnerships cost us. They waited until the storms came to ask Jonah questions they should have asked before the ship sailed."*

In the Amplified version of the Bible, these questions were, *"Who is to blame for this disaster? What is your occupation? Where do you come from? What is your country?"* (Jonah 1:8). This does not mean that we ask everyone we are friends with and intend to build something meaningful with these exact questions. What God was saying to me was, *"Be definite about who you are, what you believe in, and what your values are. Know what is important to you. Be clear about where you are going and who and what you will need to get there. When you know these things, and are about to get on any long term "ship"—courtships, relationships, friendships, and partnerships— be sure that you both stand for the same thing. You may be different in other areas, but in the things that matter most to you, you are like-minded. Otherwise, in the middle, when the storms arrive, it may be too late. There will be hurts, chaos, and pains if you do not do your work at the beginning. Though you will survive, you will have experienced losses that cost you."*

The sea did not stop its rage until Jonah was thrown off the ship. The men tried all they could to keep him on board and find their way to land. How kind of them. Still, kindness sometimes cannot stop the damaging effects of bad associations. Applying this principle, I began to choose and categorize my relationships, not because I am prideful or think I am better than others, but because I have seen through my experience, and that of others, how one person in your life with ill-intentions or actions can alter the course of your ship. The Bible puts the responsibility on us to carefully and wisely choose our relationships. Here are some words of wisdom from the Bible on relationships.

- *"Do not be misled: Bad company corrupts good character"* (1 Corinthians 15:33 NIV).
- *"Walk with the wise and become wise, for a companion of fools suffers harm"* (Proverbs 13:20 NIV).
- *"The righteous choose their friends carefully, but the way of the wicked leads them astray"* (Proverbs 12:26 NIV).

It is important that we treat people with respect, no matter how much we disagree with them. Love everyone. Jesus did. But He only took twelve closer, His disciples. Among the twelve, only three saw

Him in the intimate moments of His life—His transfiguration and His turmoil in Gethsemane. The three are Peter, James, and John. I pray for you, as I always pray for myself, that God will continually guide you with divine wisdom and counsel in choosing the people you give access into your heart, form business partnerships with, and let in on your decision-making and problem-solving, in Jesus' name. Amen.

It is important that, before we run off with directions or instructions, we know for a fact that the Spirit of God is truly our leader. We turn on the lights by opening our Bible and finding out what it says on these pressing issues. When we apply God's Word, we see that God's instructions are not for our restriction, but our protection. They are boundaries to safeguard our hearts and preserve our souls.

God's Word is like light to show us the way to go when we are in the dark, confused, and in doubt (Psalm 119:105). His Word is also likened to water, to wash us clean from sicknesses, pain, filth (Ephesians 5:26). His Word is comparable to fire that produces light for direction, heat to warm our hearts that have been hardened by cold and brutal life circumstances. It is also hot enough to remove impurities like sin, sicknesses,

> God's instructions are not for our restriction, but our protection.

anger, and unforgiveness (Jeremiah 20:9; Jeremiah 23:29). God's Word is strong like a hammer to break down the walls of fear we have built around us for our self-protection (Jeremiah 23:29). It also levels the barriers that stand on our path to the next season of our lives. His Word gives us a clear understanding of life's issues (Psalm 119:130). The Bible talks about healthy living, relationships, marriage, raising children, work ethics and all we need to live a successful life. His Word heals our pain (Psalm 107:20).

I believe the Word of God, the Bible, is absolute and complete. Whenever I doubt if it is God speaking to me, I check to see if it aligns with the Word of God and its principles before giving it a second thought. Once it scales through this, then I check it against His person. The person of God is LOVE.

The Love Test

God is described various ways in the Bible based on how the individual or group knew or experienced Him. Abraham called Him a provider, as God supplied the ram for the sacrifice (Genesis 22:14). Hagar, feeling lost and lonely in the desert, called Him Jehovah Roi, the God that sees (Genesis 16:13). To David, He was a shepherd, caretaker, guide, provider, and protector. God does many things, but there is one thing the Bible says God is, and that is love. *"The one who does not love has not become acquainted with God [does not and never did know Him], for God is love. [He is the originator of love, and it is an enduring attribute of His nature]"* (1 John 4:8 AMP).

In other words, we could say Love provides, Love protects, Love sees, because love is not just an attribute God possesses, it is who He is. Love is why He walks with us through the valley of the shadow of death. Everything He is described as, and all He does, is proof of His love for us. God never causes us pain, but He brings blessings out of our suffering and uses the process to teach us, strengthen us, and empower us to reach out to others in similar situations. Love is why He births purpose out of our pain, beauty from our ashes, because His Spirit is with us and in us. His love is impressed on us. In fact, God's love expressed through us is a significant indicator of His presence in our lives.

"By this, we know that we abide in him and he in us, because he has given us of his Spirit. And we have seen and testify that the Father has sent his Son to be the Savior of the world. Whoever confesses that Jesus is the Son of God, God abides in him, and he in God. So we have come to know and to believe the love that God has for us. God is love, and whoever abides in love abides in God, and God abides in him" (1 John 4:13-16 ESV).

"If anyone says, 'I love God,' and hates his brother, he is a liar; for he who does not love his brother whom he has seen cannot love God whom he has not seen. And this commandment we have from him: whoever loves God must also love his brother" (1 John 4:20-21 ESV).

"But the fruit of the Spirit is love, joy, peace, patience, kindness, goodness, faithfulness..." (Galatians 5:22 ESV).

Regardless of how people may treat us, use us, or be different from us, we are to show the love that God shows us. I am not saying we should expose ourselves to abusive situations, remain in these conditions, or tolerate maltreatment. Neither does loving someone mean that we keep silent when they do wrong, or when we see them headed towards disaster. Love means we speak the truth in love. Love causes us to pray for those that hurt us, for their salvation, deliverance, transformation, or whatever they may need. It is love that made Jesus die for us, even when we were yet to accept Him. Love is why we forgive those that hurt us, thereby releasing their power over us and our right to get even, even if there is no possibility of reconciliation. Love is trusting God to avenge our wrongs. The voice of the Holy Spirit does not lead us to harm but to the help for our problem.

The Power of Choice Test

The interesting thing about being guided or led by the Holy Spirit is the fact that we have the liberty to willingly follow. God does not cajole, coerce, or force us to do what He expects of us, but He needs our cooperation when He chooses to work in us and through us. Moses was frightened, and felt inadequate when God called him to lead Israel out of Egypt. In Exodus 3 and 4, we see God, in His sovereignty, persuasively nudging Moses to heed the call. When Moses drew up a list of his incompetence, God assured him. God provided help through his brother, Aaron, and also promised Moses that He would be with him.

Even Jesus cooperated with God's divine plan, all the way to the cross. People make reference to Jonah to prove that God forces us to be in His will. I believe that whatever happened to Jonah, from the ship to the belly of the fish, was an act of mercy, God's mercy. God gives us the power of choice, and the cost of not working or walking with Him is often a life of dissatisfaction, confusion, and misdirection. Still, He places the coin of obedience and disobedience in our hands. Jonah didn't reflect on His assignment or tell God why He couldn't do it, like Moses or Gideon did. He just ran away. No conversation. No pondering God's request. No questions asked. He just got up and left. Then, *"The word of the Lord came to Jonah son of Amittai: 'Go to the great city of Nineveh and preach against it, because its wickedness has come up before me.' But Jonah ran away from the Lord and headed for*

Tarshish. He went down to Joppa, where he found a ship bound for that port. After paying the fare, he went aboard and sailed for Tarshish to flee from the Lord" (Jonah 1:1-3 NIV).

God, in His ever loving nature, gave him the time and opportunity to consider his conduct carefully. It just happened to be in an unlikely place—the belly of a fish. While in this place, Jonah prayed to God in Jonah 2, and never once in that chapter did he agree to go to Ninevah, the place God had previously sent him. Instead, he had time to soberly reflect on how he got there and who God is.

God never said to him, *"Agree to go to Ninevah or remain trapped in here."* Jonah's release was not dependent on his agreement to go to Ninevah but rather on his acknowledgment of God's omnipotence. Jonah was out of the fish's stomach before the conversation about Ninevah resumed (Jonah 3).

Satan is an imitator, and similarly works through people to accomplish his purposes. Sadly, but true, there are many working for and with the devil and have no clue. The difference is that while God leads and guides, and we voluntarily follow, Satan possesses, taking dominion over the person and manipulatively controlling their power of choice. Both ways, we choose who we cooperate with, either God or Satan.

Satan searches for one willing to entertain him, because not every heart is open to him. 1 Peter 5:8 says, *"Be sober-minded; be watchful. Your adversary the devil prowls around like a roaring lion, seeking someone to devour"* (ESV). And Job 1:7 says, *"The Lord said to Satan, 'From where have you come?' Satan answered the Lord and said, 'From going to and fro on the earth, and from walking up and down on it'"* (ESV). These two scriptures reveal how Satan goes about looking for those who have their hearts open to him. We can give him access to ourselves through disobedience to God, unforgiveness, anger, resentment, fear, negative thoughts, and sin. Once entertained and engaged, he can do as much destruction as he desires based on our willingness to keep yielding to him. Yes, Satan needs our cooperation, too.

When Satan encountered Jesus, he applied a strategy as subtle as the one he used for Eve. The more we relate and spend time with someone, the more we begin to reflect them in our thinking processes, actions, responses, and reactions to circumstances. Satan understands this, so he guises his intentions as harmless thoughts. But only for a moment. He plants the seed, waters and nurtures it, until he gains a stronghold in our lives. Once he does, he takes over our mind, leaving us no room to think through our actions or their consequences. The story of Judas Iscariot is a perfect illustration of how possessive Satan can be over those who hearken to or entertain his voice or thoughts. Examine the following verses:

"It was during supper, when the devil had already put [the thought of] betraying Jesus into the heart of Judas Iscariot, Simon's son" (John 13:2 AMP).

"After [Judas had taken] the piece of bread, Satan entered him. Then Jesus said to him, 'What you are going to do, do quickly [without delay]'" (John 13:27 AMP).

Between both verses, Judas had enough time to do what Jesus did when tempted by the devil—respond with the Word. Or he could have put a halt to those thoughts, giving them no room to thrive. But he kept entertaining them, until Satan finally entered him, taking full control of him. By the time Judas came to his senses, the deed had already been done, with no chance of reversal. Or so it seemed on the surface.

God also plants a seed in our hearts. The more we water this seed, the more we resemble Him in all we do. Unlike Satan, God does not possess us when we hearken to His voice. To possess is to seize control from someone else. Instead, God gives us freewill. We have a choice—either we do what He tells us to do or we don't; either we let Him into our lives or we keep the door closed. In Revelation 3:10 God says, *"Behold, I stand at the door and knock. If anyone hears my voice and opens the door, I will come in to him and eat with him, and he with me"* (ESV).

God engages us in what He does, fostering a partnership between us. He does not force Himself on us. He leads us, expecting us to make the decision to follow. Even in His sovereignty, God does not bypass or overlook our willingness. He does not turn us into robots and then control our actions. Any voice we listen to that restricts our ability to think through its instructions is certainly not God's. Yes, there are times when God speaks and our actions need to be urgent. Still, He leaves us with the power of choice.

The Test of Conviction versus Condemnation

When Jesus lived on Earth, He put a great deal of thought into selecting those who walked with Him the most. He loved everyone, fellowshipped with some, selected twelve as His disciples, but was intimately close with only three of them—Peter, James, and John. There were miracles Jesus performed publicly for all to see, and there were also those He carried out in the presence of His twelve disciples. However, in His life, just like ours, there were intimate moments that he reserved for only a special few. In Matthew 17, Jesus climbed the mountain with His three closest disciples, and in their presence, His appearance changed. He was comfortable enough with them to reveal this aspect of His divine nature. A few chapters later, we see Jesus again with these three, but in a place of pain, the Garden of Gethsemane (Matthew 26:36-46).

We express the emotions that arise in the vulnerable seasons of our lives in the presence of those we trust the most. They can see our wounds, hear our pain, and choose to stay by our side through it. Peter, James, and John saw Jesus more than the other disciples, both in his human and divine nature. Whenever I read the story of Jesus' death, I make mental attempts to step into His shoes, and my heart bleeds at Peter's denial of Him more than His betrayal by Judas. More so because of the relationship Jesus had with Peter.

Betrayal hurts; so does rejection and denial. The degree to which we feel the pain depends highly on who the offender is. It is the one who performs the act, and not the act in itself, that causes us to feel disappointed and heartbroken. Though Jesus was aware that He was going to be betrayed by Judas and denied by Peter, He not only informed Peter but also prayed for him.

The degree to which we feel the pain depends highly on who the offender is. It is the one who performs the act, and not the act in itself, that causes us to feel disappointed and heartbroken.

"'Simon, Simon, behold, Satan demanded to have you, that he might sift you like wheat, but I have prayed for you that your faith may not fail. And when you have turned again, strengthen your brothers.' Peter said to him,

'Lord, I am ready to go with you both to prison and to death.' Jesus said, 'I tell you, Peter, the rooster will not crow this day, until you deny three times that you know me'" (Luke 22:31-34 ESV).

Assuredly, Peter gave Jesus his word. Never would he leave His side, regardless of what happened. It wasn't too long before Peter did the exact opposite of what He'd promised. As a person with feelings, just like us, I wonder how Jesus felt seeing one of His closest friends deny Him, three times. We have higher expectations of those we feel most intimate with. It is easier to think about ourselves as one slapped with the bitter experiences of rejection, denial, and betrayal than as the one who inflicts these on others. The overbearing sense of sadness on Peter led him to realize that sometimes we fail to live up to expectations.

Judas, one of the twelve, did not enjoy the privileged relationship Peter had with Jesus. When he came to himself and recognized the consequences of his actions, he went one step further to make things right.

"When Judas, His betrayer, saw that Jesus was condemned, he was gripped with remorse and returned the thirty pieces of silver to the chief priests and the elders, saying, 'I have sinned by betraying innocent blood.' They replied, 'What is that to us? See to that yourself!' And throwing the pieces of silver into the temple sanctuary, he left; and went away and hanged himself" (Matthew 27:3-5 AMP).

How could the lives of Judas and Peter have such dramatic and different outcomes, despite the similarities in their actions? Judas, full of remorse, committed suicide, while Peter put the past behind him and stepped up to the task, becoming the first leader of the church. The reason is simple: Judas was condemned, but Peter was convicted. Judas ran to man, Peter to God. Whenever we do anything that displeases God, He should be the one we go to first for healing, forgiveness, and restoration. God can truly restore our tarnished image, shattered confidence and erase our mistakes. The lives of Judas and Peter illustrate the devastating effects of condemnation and the redemptive power of conviction.

The voice of the Holy Spirit will always convict us when we make mistakes. He brings to our memory what the Bible says about the situation that faces us. He guides us into the truth—what we should have said, what we should have done, or how we could have acted—not to rub the failure or shortcoming in our faces, but to lead us to repentance and change, thereby restoring our relationship with God and others. *"For the righteous falls seven times and rises again, but the wicked stumble in times of calamity"* (Proverbs 24:16 ESV).

Conviction picks us up from where we fell under the weight of our wrongdoings and moves us closer to the source of our help—God—to help us take our eyes off the past and move forward with God into victory. Because of God, Peter was able to make progress past a disappointment into his divine appointment.

Condemnation makes us more conscious of our messes than God's available mercies towards us.

The devil speaks, and never for our good. His voice reeks of condemnation to remind us of our mistakes and failures, burdening us with guilt and blame. He paints a gory picture of the circumstances, making us lose hope for our redemption, restoration, and healing. He whispers fear in our hearts and tells us there is no way out of the mess in our lives. Condemnation makes us more conscious of our messes than God's available mercies towards us. A sense of unworthiness envelopes us, and we believe that we have not only failed ourselves but also everyone around us and God. Condemnation makes us forget that there is a God that forgives, heals, redeems, and restores. It takes us far from God. Condemnation leads us to the end Judas received. We experience death in not just our physical bodies, but our spirit and mind as well.

In seasons of life when we feel all alone and misunderstood, we should have it stamped in our hearts that the Holy Spirit is there with us. The Holy Spirit will lead us into conviction and never cause us to feel worthless. We may cry when He speaks, as we recognize where we might have erred, but we go to God's throne of mercy and grace, like Peter. We repent and go on, not remain fixated in the cycle of guilt. *"Therefore let us [with privilege] approach the throne of grace [that is, the throne of God's gracious favor] with confidence and without fear, so that we may receive mercy [for our failures] and find [His amazing] grace to help in time of need [an appropriate blessing, coming just at the right moment]"* (Hebrews 4:16 AMP).

The moment we cannot pray about our missteps and wrongdoings; we can know for sure that the spirit at work is not of God. Romans 8:1 says, *"There is therefore now no condemnation for those who are in Christ Jesus"* (ESV). So, listen carefully for that voice of conviction.

The Glory Test

Ever had your hair beautifully styled by a talented hairdresser? The edges are well defined, the curls are fluffy, and the hair extensions blend in perfectly with the natural hair. A good hairdresser knows that every well-designed hairstyle is an advertisement for potential clients. As the customer, you become a brand ambassador, showcasing the creativity of your stylist.

I entered an elevator in a corporate building, eager to get to the floor where my meeting was to take place. I could sense the intensity of the look coming from one of the elevator occupants. That look had been typical since I left my hairdresser's two days ago with my hair beautifully braided. The braids would have looked ordinary if the stylist had not invested so much attention to detail in defining the hairline to suit my facial structure and choosing the right hair extension colour to complement my skin tone.

"Your hair is lovely," I heard the lady beside me say. Before I could respond to her compliment, she added, "Where exactly did you get it done?"

I took the contact details of the hairstylist out of my purse, gave it to the lady, and when I stepped out of the elevator, all I could think of was one word, Jesus. You may ask, "What has Jesus got to do with your hair?" I'll tell you. *"For we are His workmanship [His own master work, a work of art], created in Christ Jesus [reborn from above—spiritually transformed, renewed, ready to be used] for good works, which God prepared [for us] beforehand [taking paths which He set], so that we would walk in them [living the good life which He prearranged and made ready for us]"* (Ephesians 2:10 AMP). We are God's workmanship. Like a good hairstylist, He leaves no room for flaws in His work on us. We are well thought out and beautifully designed by Him, from our smiles to our character and personality. He created us to give Him glory and not to keep it to ourselves (Isaiah 43:7). We are

129

His advertisement, displaying His magnificence everywhere we go. *"But thanks be to God, who in Christ always leads us in triumphal procession, and through us spreads the knowledge of the fragrance of him everywhere"* (2 Corinthians 2:14 ESV).

To be His brand ambassadors, God first glorifies us, just like the hairdresser beautifies us with her talent. Now we look beautiful, and that beauty points others to the one who did the work. We are that masterpiece. God is that stylist. The Holy Spirit will make known to us things that will improve us and cause God to be exalted. Our lives can only give God glory to the extent to which we allow ourselves to be glorified by Him.

> To be His brand ambassadors, God first glorifies us, just like the hairdresser beautifies us with her talent.

"When Jesus had spoken these words, he lifted up his eyes to heaven, and said, 'Father, the hour has come; glorify your Son that the Son may glorify you. I glorified you on earth, having accomplished the work that you gave me to do. And now, Father, glorify me in your own presence with the glory that I had with you before the world existed'" (John 17:1, 4-5 ESV).

In the difficult seasons of our lives, God intervenes in ways that confirm His presence with us—a word of encouragement to keep us moving forward, just when we are about to hit the brakes; a financial need met; and restored relationships. He also uses us, even in these dark times, to reach out to others in need. When people see you encouraging others at a time when your world is turned upside down and you could use some yourself, and when He uses the little you have to be a big blessing to someone else, He glorifies you and He is glorified as well. The people see you and appreciate your obedience, courage, and generosity, but they give glory to God for you, for an answered prayer, for a provision met, or for the right word spoken at the right time. We should be wary of giving a listening ear to any voice or leading where we become the "hairstylist," taking credit for what God has done.

One great example of giving God glory is the testing of Jesus in the wilderness. After two failed attempts by Satan to get Jesus to do his bidding—the first, asking him to command stones to turn to bread, and the second, bowing to him—Satan decided to give it one more shot.

"Then he led Jesus to Jerusalem and had Him stand on the pinnacle (highest point) of the temple, and said [mockingly] to Him, 'If You are the Son of God, throw Yourself down from here; for it is written and forever remains written, 'He will command His angels concerning You to guard and protect You,' and, 'they will lift You up on their hands, So that You do not strike Your foot against a stone.' Jesus replied to him, "It is said [in Scripture], 'you shall not tempt the Lord your God [to prove Himself to you]'" (Luke 4:9-12 AMP).

Jesus knew that we are supposed to live in obedience to God at all times. Yes, He had the capacity to turn those stones into bread, but was God the Father going to be praised by that act? Or was it going to showcase the prophetic prowess of Jesus? God would not get any glory or honour from those actions if Jesus had heeded to Satan's instructions. Satan made it look like he wanted Jesus to have those things, but beneath his facade was an attempt to make God appear irrelevant in the fulfillment of Jesus' destiny. We need to ensure that our actions are not rooted in self-glorification for it's often the enemy that directs and guides us down this path.

The Peace Test

"Let me hear what God the Lord will speak, for he will speak peace to his people, to his saints; but let them not turn back to folly" (Psalm 85:8 ESV).

In Isaiah 9:6, we see the prophet Isaiah refer to Jesus as the Prince of Peace when he prophesied His coming. *"For to us a child is born, to us a son is given, and the government will be on his shoulders. And he will be called Wonderful Counselor, Mighty God, Everlasting Father, Prince of Peace"* (Isaiah 9: 6 NIV).

Man's relationship with God became strained after Adam and Eve fell out with God because of their act of disobedience. Jesus came to restore that relationship. It takes a person of peace to bring a permanent resolution to a long-standing conflict. Since Jesus embodied peace, it should be no surprise that even in the midst of a storm, He was soundly asleep.

"And a great windstorm arose, and the waves were breaking into the boat, so that the boat was already filling. But he was in the stern, asleep on the cushion. And they woke him and said to him, 'Teacher, do you not care that we are perishing?' And he awoke and rebuked the wind and said to the sea, 'Peace! Be still!' And the wind ceased, and there was a great calm" (Mark 4:37-39 ESV).

Peace does not mean that all around us is well. It means that all is well within us, regardless of what eclipses us. It was the peace on the inside of Jesus that He extended to His turbulent environment. We cannot hear the Holy Spirit with our hearts burdened and disturbed. Peace is a reminder of His presence with us, our circumstances notwithstanding.

I facilitate training sessions and workshops regularly, and as time went on, the number of participants attending the sessions increased. I became afraid and began asking myself, "What if I forget what I am meant to say? What if someone asks me a question I have no answers to?" Fear, indeed, is paralyzing, because the moment these thoughts came and I entertained them, I became apprehensive in the course of my preparation. One day, I was studying my materials for an upcoming presentation. The audience was going to be larger than my previous workshops.

"You are going to mess this up," I heard the enemy tell me. "You will forget your lines," he said tauntingly.

I became nervous.

Suddenly, the Holy Spirit said to me, *"Do you know that before Jesus died, Peter had never spoken to a large audience? He was bold enough to engage Jesus in conversations and ask Him questions, but he never had a large public audience."*

Then He brought to my mind that in Peter's first public speech, three thousand people repented. *"Peter could do this because he had Me—the Holy Spirit. Osayi, you have Me, too."*

That scripture quieted my unsettled heart. I came to the conclusion that my heart was at rest, not because my conditions changed, but because my confidence in God had increased. I spoke so eloquently and boldly at the conference, injecting humour when needed, and received great and positive feedback from the organizers. It was my 'Godfidence' at work.

I later read the story in Acts 2. The Holy Spirit came upon the disciples after Jesus ascended to Heaven, just as Jesus had promised. Peter was one of these disciples. It was immediately after this encounter that he addressed the crowd. Obviously, there were more than three thousand people present, although that was the number that gave their lives to Christ.

"Let the peace of Christ [the inner calm of one who walks daily with Him] be the controlling factor in your hearts [deciding and settling questions that arise]. To this peace indeed you were called as members in one body [of believers]. And be thankful [to God always]" (Colossians 3:15 AMP).

How did I make the switch from Jesus to the Holy Spirit? The Holy Spirit is the Spirit of Peace, for peace is a fruit found in the life of believers who have the Holy Spirit (Galatians 5:22). So, He can give us peace. Jesus is the Word, the Word that became flesh. If Jesus is the Prince of Peace, it means that we can find peace in the Word, for that's who He is. A troubled heart cannot receive divine signals, as it operates in a realm different from that of the Holy Spirit. That is why we are told to be still and know that God is God (Psalm 46:10). In other words, let what is written in the Bible, the Word of God, bring peace and calmness to our souls. Sometimes, we seek the peace that is not of God. But there is a big difference between the peace we get from God, and from the world.

"Peace I leave with you; my peace I give to you. Not as the world gives do I give to you. Let not your hearts be troubled, neither let them be afraid" (John 14:27 ESV).

Peace in the world is short-lived, as the world is ever changing. Policies change. Global markets rise and fall. Leaders change. World peace is dependent on what is external. Such peace comes when the economy develops, the bank accounts are full, or we meet someone new for a promising relationship. And if these fail, the peace goes with it. Godly peace is security in Christ, for He never changes (Malachi 3:6). His peace is steady and stable; a deep-rooted assurance and trust in who and what the Word of God says about us.

The peace of God keeps us at ease in the midst of turbulent situations. We see a good example of this in the story of Paul's trip to Rome. In Acts 21:11, the Holy Spirit had spoken to Paul, through a prophet, about the trials ahead of him (Acts 21:11). The message came, not to discourage Paul but to prepare him and make him undisturbed, even in life threatening situations. Two chapters after, the Lord visited Paul and said to him, *"Take courage! As you have testified about me in Jerusalem, so you must also testify in Rome"* (Acts 23: 11 NIV). Because Paul had heard from God that he will testify about Him God in Rome, he was confident in the face of future challenges. On the way to Rome, a storm arose and the ship sailed in the direction of the forceful wind. Everyone feared for their lives, except Paul. Paul was calm, for He had heard the voice of God. He said to the others in the ship, *"I have faith in God that it will happen just as he told me"* (Acts 27:25). He was unmoved by the circumstances, and that rest distinguished. Paul spoke hope to them and encouraged them to have some food (Acts 27:33-36).

I find that when I am uneasy about a decision, and I go ahead anyway, I end up being regretful. We can be peaceful, even if we appear visibly afraid to take a step. Peace is in the heart, and if we allow it to take root, it later overshadows whatever fear, doubt, or anxiety we have. Listen deep down for the Holy Spirit to speak peace. These are guides to identify when the Holy Spirit is leading us or speaking to us. When at a crossroads and I do not know what

to do, I search within me for peace. Peace will always lead anything that is Holy Spirit driven, even if we sense inadequacy or fear.

*"For you shall go out in joy and be led forth in peace; the moun-
tains and the hills before you shall break forth into singing, and
all the trees of the field shall clap their hands"* (Isaiah 55:12 ESV).

———————◉———————

These are guidelines on how the Holy Spirit communicates
to us, and with us. We cannot restrict how God speaks to us, but
I know that His voice will never contradict His Word. He is not
a man whose utterances can be easily swayed or become subject to public opinion. God's Word is His integrity, and the Bible
records that He exalts His Word above all His names (Psalm 138:2).
Whatever God says will also give us peace, for He is called the God
of Peace (Hebrews 13:20; Romans 15:33; 2 Thessalonians 3:16).

*"Great peace have those who love your law, and nothing can
make them stumble"* (Psalm 119:165 NIV). Loving God's Word
gives us peace. Even if you are uncertain about a decision, let His
Word and His peace be your guide.

Chapter Eight

COME CLOSER

"Abraham believed God, and it was counted to him as righteousness" —and he was called a friend of God" (James 2:23b ESV).

THE BIBLE STARTS off with God's creation of the heavens and the earth. God began to speak and bring into existence what He wanted. *"And God said, "Let there be an expanse [of the sky] in the midst of the waters, and let it separate the waters [below the expanse] from the waters [above the expanse]." And God made the expanse [of sky] and separated the waters which were under the expanse from the waters which were above the expanse; and it was so [just as He commanded]"* (Genesis 1:6-7 AMP). God created the world and everything in it in six days.

In Genesis 1:26, God proclaimed His intent to create man in His image, and got to work. God had great plans and assignments for man, and wasted no time in declaring His expectations. It is like starting a job on the first day and having your responsibilities laid out for you. Genesis 1:27-30 says, *"So God created man in his own image, in the image of God he created him; male and female he created them. And God blessed them. And God said to them, 'Be fruitful and multiply and fill the earth and subdue it, and have dominion over the fish of the sea and over the birds of the heavens and over every living thing that moves on the earth.' And God said, 'Behold, I have given you every plant yielding seed that is on the face of all the earth, and every tree with seed in its fruit. You shall have them for food. And to every beast of the earth and to every bird of the heavens and to everything that creeps on the earth, everything that has the breath of life, I have given every green plant for food.' And it was so"* (ESV).

Man was not the only creation God made. God regularly went back to meet with man, not only to inspect and keep track of what He'd asked him to do, but also to fellowship with him. In Genesis 2:18, God said, *"It is not good for the man to be alone. I will make a helper suitable for him"* (NIV). The next thing God did was to bring the animals for Adam to name and after he did so, the Bible recorded that *"no suitable helper was found for him"* (Genesis 2: 20b NIV). God then put Adam to sleep and took out of him the female that already existed in him. And Adam called her *woman. "And the rib that the Lord God had taken from the man he made into a woman and brought her to the man. Then the man said, 'This at last is bone of my bones and flesh of my flesh; she shall be called Woman, because she was taken out of Man'"* (Genesis 2:22-23 ESV).

When Adam and his wife, Eve ate a fruit from the tree God had forbidden them from eating, the Bible records that at the sound of God's steps, they went into hiding. *"And they heard the sound of the LORD God walking in the garden in the cool of the day, and the man and his wife hid themselves from the presence of the LORD God among the trees of the garden"* (Genesis 3:8 ESV). Adam and

Eve were yet to see Him, but due to the familiarity of the sound of His strides, they recognized His presence. It is evident that God always visited them in the Garden of Eden, because of all the things He created, these two were His most treasured investment. Surely, God cares about the plants and animals, but Adam and Eve were the only ones that had what the others didn't have—His image. *"So God created man in his own image, in the image of God he created him; male and female he created them* (Genesis 1: 27 ESV). They were a reflection of Him for they had not only His image but His breath as well. Genesis 2: 7 says God breathed into the nostrils of man the breath of life, and he had life. Nothing could separate them from God. Romans 8:38-39 says, *"For I am convinced [and continue to be convinced— beyond any doubt] that neither death, nor life, nor angels, nor principalities, nor things present and threatening, nor things to come, nor powers, nor height, nor depth, nor any other created thing, will be able to separate us from the [unlimited] love of God, which is in Christ Jesus our Lord"* (AMP).

> God cannot leave us alone, for we are in His image and are carriers of His presence.

We, like Adam and Eve, are very important to God. God cannot leave us alone, for we are in His image and are carriers of His presence.

In Genesis 18, Abraham received three guests. One was God, and the other two were His angels. They appeared in human form to Abraham and Sarah, who entertained them with food. As they departed, God thought to Himself in verse 17 (NIV), *"Shall I hide from Abraham what I am about to do?"* Why should I keep away from him such relevant information?" God and His angels were on their way to Sodom and Gomorrah to see for themselves if the outcry that had reached Heaven concerning these cities were true. After God unveiled His agenda to Abraham, Abraham had the privilege of negotiating the salvation of Sodom and Gomorrah with God. Amazing! No wonder he was called the friend of God.

We are not different today from Abraham and the numerous people God interacted with in the Bible. We, like them, are His children, and God still desires to be close to and commune with us. In relationships, we nurture one another to maintain intimacy, and our connection with God is not an exception.

In Romans 8: 38 – 39 we see the many things that can never put a stumbling block between God and us. *"For I am convinced [and continue to be convinced—beyond any doubt] that neither death, nor life, nor angels, nor principalities, nor things present and threatening, nor things to come, nor powers, nor height, nor depth, nor any other created thing, will be able to separate us from the [unlimited] love of God, which is in Christ Jesus our Lord"* (AMP).

However, there is one critical factor that was not listed but has the potential of separating us from God—you and me. We have the power to do this by our actions, decisions, inactions, and choices that can result in a detachment in our relationship with God. We all know what happened with Adam and Eve. They lost their place in the Garden of Eden through an act of disobedience to God.

According to the New Testament, everyone who confesses Jesus as their Lord and Saviour receives the Holy Spirit. He is a gift from God to believers, for God has promised never to leave us (Acts 2:38). Nevertheless, we could grieve and quench His presence in our lives. Ever seen a couple that just lives together but has lost the spark of two people in love? That is what our lives look like when we ruin the fellowship we have with God. In Chapter Five, I talked about the grieving and quenching of the Holy Spirit. It is our responsibility to keep the intimacy between God and us alive. He's taken the first step by sending the Holy Spirit to be with us. How we reciprocate will determine the fruitfulness of our relationship with Him. It is important to say here that it is in our seeking a relationship with God that we discover His presence. Think about it. In reality, the people whose presence in our lives are meaningful are those we have spent time cultivating and nurturing a relationship with.

The enemy's best tactic is deception, and everything he does is unoriginal and a cheap fabrication of God's ideas and strategies. Not taking the time to know God personally can make us vulnerable to Satan's manipulation and deception. But when we come closer, it becomes easy to identify God's presence and voice, and fish out what is not His.

We draw nearer to God in many ways:

Obedience

In John 15:14, Jesus says, *"You are my friends if you do what I command"* (NIV). When you obey the instructions someone gives you, it depicts your respect for them. It says, "I honour you enough to do what you ask of me." Disobedience is total disregard, not just of the directive given, but of the person issuing it. God detests disobedience.

Whenever God asks us to do something, either a commandment already in the Bible or an instruction He's given to us by revelation, the persons who stands to benefit from it is us, not God. We are the only benefactors of our obedience to God. You know why God is not the benefactor? It is because He can always use another person to carry out His instruction. If that happens, we are the ones that lose out. The more we disobey His commands, the more we become less sensitive to His leading, resulting in what the Bible calls "a hardened heart" (Acts 28:26-28). The longer we delay obedience, the more we display a rebellious attitude towards God.

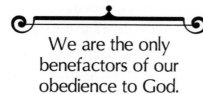

We are the only benefactors of our obedience to God.

Instant obedience, once you have settled in your heart that the Holy Spirit is indeed leading you, is one way of showing your love for Him. The more we do this, the more our hearts gladden at His commands, and the more He delights in communicating with us. *"We know that we have come to know him if we keep his commands"* (1 John 2:3 NIV).

We do not get God's love by our obedience. He already loved us while we were deeply engrossed in sin. By our obedience, God knows His love is reciprocated. Our obedience is the instrument that draws us closer to Him, and the nearer we are to Him, the more our lives reflect Him. Through that flow of intimacy, we become His fruit bearers. And these fruits are true markers that we have the Holy Spirit in our lives. Matthew 7:16 tells us, *"You will recognize them by their fruits. Are grapes gathered from thornbushes, or figs from thistles?"* (ESV).

The same way our obedience bridges the gap between the Holy Spirit and us, our disobedience works to distance us from Him. Abraham did not just become a friend of God overnight. He obeyed His way to such a revered position. God brought Abraham out of an idolatrous family. Likewise, He has called us out of sin—lying, gossip, adultery, fornication, theft, and more. Abraham started out with God on the same level playing field as many of us. We even have a better covenant in Jesus Christ, and yet, not many of us can boast of the type of relationship Abraham had with God. As Abraham complied with every instruction God gave Him, the closer his relationship with God became. This obedience-based relationship culminated in the blessing of Abraham that we are now beneficiaries of when we believe in Jesus (Galatians 3:29).

The Holy Spirit did not permanently dwell with people in the Old Testament but came upon those appointed by God for a particular task. It is in light of this that the Holy Spirit left Saul when He consistently disobeyed God's instructions. In the New Testament, the Holy Spirit is a promise from God that we will never be alone. And I believe God is a promise keeper. However, we can grieve or quench the Holy Spirit's presence in our life by our inactions, sinful actions, disobedience, and disregard for His presence. It does not mean that He leaves us, but we make His presence of no effect. We are the ones that miss out on a rewarding and exciting relationship if this happens. We can restore that relationship by humbly asking God for forgiveness and obeying His commandments.

Anytime I feel distant from God, I check myself first. Am I working in obedience to God as commanded in the Scriptures? Are there instructions God has given me that I have paid little or no attention to? In the desert seasons of life, our response to what God requires of us is crucial. It could be giving out to others when we are short of resources ourselves. It could be taking the first step towards reconciliation, even when we are the aggrieved ones. Sometimes, the first step is not to restore the relationship but to begin the process of the inner-healing we need.

Whatever steps of obedience we believe God has given us, it is advisable to weigh them against His Word, His character, and His peace. God will never lead us to destruction, of ourselves or of others. As we obey, we are drawn nearer to the source of our hope.

The Word

"But what does it say? 'The word is near you, in your mouth and in your heart' (that is, the word of faith that we proclaim)" (Romans 10:8 ESV).

The scripture above tells us where the Word of God should be in us, namely in our mouth and in our heart. Many of us see the Word with our eyes and stop right there. It is what we do with the Word that we see that impacts us. We are not only to read the Word, but to speak it, think about it, and live it out. Remember, the Word is Jesus, and until we say it as God did, we will never see its potency in our lives.

To get the Word in our heart, we have to meditate on it. Biblical meditation differs from many kinds of meditation techniques out there. We do not require a special place or position. All we need to do is take the Word and gradually think about it. Since Jesus is the Word, imagine what this does to our mind, our ways, our behaviour, and our relationship with the Holy Spirit when we constantly have Jesus on our lips and heart.

When I read the Bible, the verse that strikes me the most spends the day with me. In my spare time, I begin to meditate on that verse. What does it mean? In what context was it spoken? How does it apply to me or my present situation? As I do this, I realize that my imagination opens up. I begin to see how this Word fits with my life. The Holy Spirit inspired the Word movement, from Heaven to the pen of man, giving us the Bible. The more I meditate, the more I work with the Holy Spirit in understanding the truths in the Scripture as it applies to me and my situation, thus building a connection between us.

To understand biblical meditation, think of the animals that ruminate. There may be no grass or vegetation nearby, but you see them sitting down, relaxed and chewing. They bring out of their belly what they had previously eaten, and chew on it, again. The more we keep the Word before us by reading it, in us by meditating on it, and on our lips by speaking it, the deeper our intimacy with the Holy Spirit becomes. David, a lover of God, always delighted when He found God's Word (Psalm 119:162). It was as good as finding God Himself. Jeremiah was a prophet that found God's words and the pleasure in them. To find connotes there was a searching done. It means they made deliberate efforts to find them.

"Your words were found, and I ate them, and your words became to me a joy and the delight of my heart, for I am called by your name, O Lord, God of hosts" (Jeremiah 15:16 ESV)

Now we have this same word, in print and electronic formats. We have apps to remind us to come closer to God every day. Are we taking advantage of the privileges we have to develop our relationship with God through the Word?

Praise

"Enter His gates with a song of thanksgiving and His courts with praise. Be thankful to Him, bless and praise His name" (Psalm 100:4 AMP).

It may seem absurd to praise God when our world is falling apart and we cannot seem to make sense of it, but when we praise God, we exalt Him above ourselves and our circumstances. We are saying that regardless of what's happened, or is currently swirling around us, God's still God. According to the *Webster's Revised Unabridged Dictionary*, praise is "to commend; to applaud; to express approbation of; to laud; applied to a person or his acts."[2] By this definition, it may seem weird to praise God when threatened by a health challenge, or when the bills are yet to be paid, or when a loved one walks away, or when faced with legal battles on all fronts. Telling God He is mighty and worthy amid these things sounds unrealistic.

The psalmist David had his share of challenges that appeared as though God had abandoned him. He cried out in Psalm 22:1-2, *"My God, my God, why hast thou forsaken me? why art thou so far from helping me, and from the words of my roaring? O my God, I cry in the day time, but thou hearest not; and in the night season, and am not silent"* (KJV). Feeling hopeless, he cried out to God around the clock, day and night. Still, it appeared that God did not hear him. Suddenly, he had an *aha* moment. This God whose presence he desired now, dwelt in the midst of praise. *"But thou art holy, O thou inhabitest the praises of Israel"* (Psalm 22:3 KJV).

Praise acknowledges God for who He is. *"But thou art holy,"* the psalmist says. It is a great joy to be loved for who you are. God is faithful, even if I lose faith in these overwhelming situations. God is love, despite the hate and rejection I have encountered. God is with me and for me in the face of injustice, betrayal, divorce, death of a loved one, miscarriage, and dwindling accounts. My circumstances may change, but God remains the same. Praise applauds God for what He's done in times past. Praise says, "I know You can do today what You have previously done."

In Psalm 22: 4 – 5, David said, *"Our fathers trusted in thee: they trusted, and thou didst deliver them. They cried unto thee, and were delivered: they trusted in thee, and were not confounded"* (Psalm 22:4-5 KJV). Remembering what God's done before, praise says, "I know You can even do more." Praise is hopeful.

Continuing from verses 6 to 18, David records how despised, rejected, and mocked he was by others. His soul was anguished; and he was left alone, as he said in verse 11, *"Be not far from me; for trouble is near; for there is none to help"* (KJV).

Finally, David cried out to God for help, *"But be not thou far from me, O Lord: O my strength, haste thee to help me. Deliver my soul from the sword; my darling from the power of the dog. Save me from the lion's mouth: for thou hast heard me from the horns of the unicorns"* (Psalm 22:19-21 KJV). David decided to do what His ancestors did. They praised God when they could not find Him in their circumstances. They praised God when they did not know what to do. They glorified and honoured God when faced with life battles.

David chose to give God the recognition He deserved, despite his turmoil. He said, *"I will declare thy name unto my brethren: in the midst of the congregation will I praise thee. Ye that fear the Lord, praise him; all ye the seed of Jacob, glorify him; and fear him, all ye the seed of Israel"* (Psalm 22:22-23 KJV). This praise he gave God until the end of Psalm 22. After Psalm 22, where we see an overwhelmed David, desperate for a change, comes his next psalm—Psalm 23. Psalm 23 is filled with the presence of God as David's provider, protector, guide, companion, and leader. We see God bring peace to one who was formerly troubled. The same situation that David thought would swallow him was what God walked him through, correcting and comforting him as they went. In the very presence of those who wanted to take David down, God reciprocated the glory and praise David had given Him earlier by preparing a banquet-sized blessing for him (Psalm 23). God did these because of the praise and honour David had given Him.

There are many ways to praise God in the Scriptures: with a dance and with instruments, as seen in the case of Miriam and the Israelites after the exodus from Egypt (Exodus 15:20-21) and as David danced before the Lord (2 Samuel 6:14-15; Psalm 149: 3); with words, exalting who He is and what He's done, as when Hannah glorified God after the birth of Samuel (1 Samuel 2:1-10); with a song, as instructed in Ephesians 5:19 and demonstrated by Paul and Silas in Acts 16:25. Our testimonies praise God too, when we recount and tell others what He has done and is doing in our lives.

Remember, the Holy Spirit is God—His Spirit with us and in us. He is already present in the life of the believer. When we glorify or praise Him, we endear ourselves to Him. He already loves us. Praise is our way of telling God how much we adore Him. This action moves us nearer to Him. Everyone enjoys the company of those who celebrate them rather than tolerate them. We do not bask in the presence of those who complain about us and find faults with our person and our doings. As we honour Him through our praise, He gravitates towards us, tightening our bond with Him.

Forgiveness

"But to you who are listening I say: Love your enemies, do good to those who hate you, bless those who curse you, pray for those who mistreat you" (Luke 6:27-28 NIV).

One time, I saw myself in a dream, going up a mountain and carrying many bags. I would get to a certain point and fall, rolling all the way back to my starting point. I cannot recall precisely the number of times I fell, though it was more than once. Finally, I gave up and sat at the base of the mountain with my bags, crying. A man came towards me and asked me to give him my bags. Holding tightly to my stuff, I turned the other way and continued crying. He later said to me, "You cannot go far with all these weights. Give them to me so you can move up." Reluctantly, I did and began to climb. It was easier this time around. There was no falling. No rolling over. I kept going forward until I awoke.

That dream never made sense to me, until God began speaking to me about unclogging my heart. He would tell me the people He wanted me to call and either forgive or ask for forgiveness. It was not fun and not what I would naturally do, but as I obeyed, I saw that it was more about me than them. For God could not reach me, and I could not get close to Him, with these obstacles that would drown out His voice. It is only after we unburden ourselves that we can have a free and unhindered relationship with God.

Unforgiveness steals our moment from us. We invest the energy and time that should be spent on productive and meaningful ventures into carrying the weights of unforgiveness and making excuses for their existence. Unforgiveness adds a few pounds to our spiritual weight. It blocks the flow of intimacy between God and us. It is also pride to hold onto and carry grudges against others. When we do so, we are telling God, "I can handle this on my own. I can avenge myself. I will repay." No matter how hard we try, we can never do God's job for Him. It wears us out emotionally, spiritually, mentally, and then it begins to show in our physical bodies.

"Beloved, never avenge yourselves, but leave it to the wrath of God, for it is written, 'Vengeance is mine, I will repay, says the Lord'" (Romans 12:19 ESV).

I know that there are cases where we look up and say, "God, how do You expect me to forgive after how I have been hurt?" It appears challenging. However, when we remember the times when God has shown us mercy, it helps us extend that mercy to others.

"But love your enemies, do good to them, and lend to them without expecting to get anything back. Then your reward will be great, and you will be children of the Most High, because he is kind

to the ungrateful and wicked. Be merciful, just as your Father is merciful" (Luke 6:35-36 NIV).

We also need to realize that receiving forgiveness from God is tied to our ability to let go of the wrongs others have done to us. Yes, forgiveness is a commandment from God. *"And forgive us our debts, as we have forgiven our debtors [letting go of both the wrong and the resentment]. For if you forgive others their trespasses [their reckless and willful sins], your heavenly Father will also forgive you. But if you do not forgive others [nurturing your hurt and anger with the result that it interferes with your relationship with God], then your Father will not forgive your trespasses"* (Matthew 6:12, 14, 15 AMP).

The story of Joseph is one that would have ended differently if many of us were in his shoes—betrayed, lied upon, falsely accused, and imprisoned. I mean, he had every right to stack up on anger, bitterness, and resentment. The journey of his pain began because of his father's special love for him, a love that set him apart from his brothers. To top it all, the young man had dreams of his future wherein his brothers and parents bowed to him. Why he shared the information with his family, we will never know. Perhaps, he is like those of us who love to dish out the exciting details of our lives to those we love and trust the most. I can be like that sometimes. Sadly, not everyone sees the big picture as we do and sometimes the subject of our discussion with loved ones can suddenly become an object in their hands for our destruction. Rather than help you build, they tear you down, with words and actions.

Still, whenever the enemy would thrust Joseph down, he would not go down alone. God was with him—in the pit where his brothers kept him before selling him; in Potiphar's house where his love and fear of God were greater than the desire to satisfy the sexual hunger of Potiphar's wife; and within the confines of the prison where he was locked up due to the false accusation of Potiphar's wife. God went everywhere with him.

Ever done the right thing and ended up with bigger problems on your hands? And at the same time God feels so far away. In reality, however, He is there, watching you, protecting you, shielding you, and ordering your steps, even when it does not appear to be so. We are never to use our emotions as a yardstick to determine God's presence. His Word says He is always with us. We just need to accept the truth, which is what God says.

I believe God went all the way with Joseph because of his heart. Never was it recorded that Joseph was full of anger and rage. Many of us would be counting our days to come out of prison, utilizing every moment of our jail time to plot our payback. However, all Joseph was concerned about was his release, not what to do to his haters when he got out. It was in this season that God fine-tuned his gifts and talents. Joseph the dreamer who could not interpret the dreams he had as a teenager became Joseph the dream interpreter. His dreams became a reality, and Joseph was ruler over the entire land, next in command only to Pharaoh himself. This put Joseph in charge of the very man who placed him in prison, namely Potiphar. Potiphar was only an officer and guard captain to Pharaoh while Joseph was the most powerful leader, after Pharaoh. Yet, with all his authority, he never got even with Potiphar, nor did he repay his brothers for their ill-treatment of him when he came face to face with them, again.

"But Joseph said to them, 'Do not fear, for am I in the place of God? As for you, you meant evil against me, but God meant it for

good, to bring it about that many people should be kept alive, as they are today'" (Genesis 50:19-20 ESV).

His perspective in the above verse weeded out unforgiveness, bitterness, and resentment, creating an atmosphere for God's presence to dwell. Hebrews 12:14-15 tells us to *"Strive for peace with everyone, and for the holiness without which no one will see the Lord. See to it that no one fails to obtain the grace of God; that no 'root of bitterness' springs up and causes trouble, and by it many become defiled"* (ESV). See every opportunity to wallow in unforgiveness, bitterness, and resentment as a chance to destroy your relationship with the Holy Spirit. Instead of giving the enemy a foothold, ask the Holy Spirit for help to forgive and let go. It is a spiritual instruction that you cannot do in the power of the flesh. If we look at it the other way around, perhaps it was the presence of God that prevented Joseph from becoming hardened in bitterness, for God knew unforgiveness and bitterness would do him more harm than good.

If you struggle with forgiving others and letting go of hurts, please say this prayer:

Sweet Holy Spirit, my ever-present help, comforter, and strength, I invite you into my life to help me forgive those that have used me, hurt me, lied to me, and betrayed me. I ask that your power be made available to me to walk in obedience to your commandments. I release every pain they have caused me. By your power, give me an exchange according to your word in Isaiah 61. Take away every pain, and give me peace. Let every spirit of heaviness, bitterness, and unforgiveness in my life give way right now to the spirit of joy, beauty, and peace. Teach me how to shrug off offences easily, so they have no chance of taking root in me. Help me to rest in your love for me and your promise to right my every wrong. Help me, Holy Spirit, to walk in your ways and your will for my life, in Jesus' name I pray. Amen.

Offering and Sacrifice

Though an offering can be likened to a sacrifice, they are symbolically different. In both cases, we release our resources, time, talents, presence, and more for the benefit of others and the promotion of God's Kingdom. It is a way of putting the things we value where our hearts are (Matthew 6:21). When we are a blessing to the church, the people of God and the needs of the church as an institution, as well as humanity, we become a blessing to God. In Matthew 25: 40, Jesus says that *"whatever you did for one of the least of these brothers and sisters of mine, you did it for me"* (NIV). However, sacrifice requires more than the dissemination of resources or the application of skills. We give up temporary pleasures to gain permanent blessings. It costs us, stretches our faith muscles, and is usually inconvenient.

Sacrifice takes more than willingness to give. It requires the grace of God and His power at work in us, to see everything we have as a medium to express His love to others. *"Now, brothers and sisters, we want to tell you about the grace of God which has been evident in the churches of Macedonia [awakening in them a longing to contribute]; for during an ordeal of severe distress, their abundant joy and their deep poverty [together] overflowed in the wealth of their lavish generosity. For I testify that according to their ability, and beyond their ability, they gave voluntarily,*

begging us insistently for the privilege of participating in the ser-
vice for [the support of] the saints [in Jerusalem]. Not only [did
they give materially] as we had hoped, but first they gave them-
selves to the Lord and to us [as His representatives] by the will of
God [disregarding their personal interests and giving as much as
they possibly could]" (2 Corinthians 8:1-5 AMP).

In the above scripture, it says that they gave according to their
ability, meaning that we give from what we have. We do not get
into debt to make offerings or sacrifice to the Lord; it has to be
within our means. But then again, it says that the Macedonian
church gave beyond their ability. At this point, their contributions
went above offerings and became a sacrifice, in the sense that it
exceeded what they ordinarily would have provided.

All sacrifices are offerings, but not all offerings are sacrificial. If someone has one hundred dollars and can comfortably give
twenty dollars, it is an offering and is within their means. Once
the person surpasses twenty dol-
lars to the maximum they have, it
becomes sacrificial. Additionally,
the Macedonian church gave, not
only materially to the individuals

All sacrifices are offerings, but not all offerings are sacrificial.

in need, but also spiritually to the Lord first. For when we do good
deeds without having a heart for God, it may have earthly benefit
but is eternally meaningless.

Our offerings and sacrifices draw us nearer to God, who is
already with us and in us. When God wanted to connect personally
with humans again after the fall of Adam, He sacrificially offered
His only Son, Jesus Christ, as the penance for our sins. It was an
offering, for He gave willingly, and a sacrifice, for it cost Him His

son's life. Today, Jesus is the bridge between God the Father and us. It took this much for God to get as close to us as He was in the Garden of Eden. Also, Jesus willingly gave up His life for us to have a relationship with God. If the Creator of the universe had to make a sacrifice to be close to us, then we need to show Him we appreciate what He's done for us.

Please, in no way does this mean we have to take our lives to get close to God, for God doesn't like murder and suicide. Remember, we never do anything to earn God's love, but we take actions to express our gratitude for His love for us. One cannot love without making investments in whom or what they love. Love is sacrificial. It is a matter of choice more than convenience. The death of Jesus on the cross was not convenient. He made a choice, and took an action, motivated by His love for us.

In the Old Testament, King Solomon sacrificially offered the Lord a thousand burnt offerings, and this act provoked God's visit to Him. At the time, it was normal to give animals to the Lord. Solomon did this for no reason other than His love for God (1 Kings 3:3a). In response to Solomon's display of his love for God, God offered him the opportunity to ask Him for anything his heart desired. Solomon asked for wisdom. After granting his request, God entered into a covenant with Solomon and promised to give him long life, if only Solomon walked in His ways and obeyed Him like his father, David, did (1 Kings 3:14). Solomon knew how to give his possessions to God and the people, but he failed critically in one area—the sacrifice of the heart.

His father, David, said in Psalm 51:16-17, *"For you will not delight in sacrifice, or I would give it; you will not be pleased with a burnt offering. The sacrifices of God are a broken spirit;*

a broken and contrite heart, O God, you will not despise" (ESV). This is an excerpt from David's prayer to God after he slept with Bathsheba, who was married to Uriah, one of David's soldiers. When Bathsheba found out she was pregnant, David tried to get Uriah to return home so he could sleep with his wife, and thus become responsible for her pregnancy. It was a time of war, and Uriah's commitment to David and Israel's safety was greater than his desire for intimacy with his wife. Unable to persuade him, David strategized the death of a man who was loyal to his well-being, and ended up marrying his wife. David hid his sins, but God fished them out. The child Bathsheba bore died, and God later blessed them with another son, Solomon. David knew that to offer anything to God, no matter how expensive, without first offering his heart in repentance and obedience to God was a waste of time and effort.

God desires us to be broken before being used. Being broken rids us of self and fills us with Him. A person with a broken heart and spirit is one who willingly obeys God, absolutely trusts God, understand their human limitation and completely abide in God's infinite ability, and lives a holy and sacrificial life.

David sacrificed his heart as he did his possessions, and enjoyed God's presence and protection. In the New Testament, Jesus paid the price and, thankfully, animal offerings and sacrifices are no longer needed. Imagine what our Sunday services in church would look like, with everyone carrying the sheep, rams, and more to the altar. Still, the sacrifice of our heart is needed today as it was back then. Hebrews 13:15 says, *"Through Jesus, therefore, let us continually offer to God a sacrifice of praise—the fruit of lips that openly profess his name"* (NIV). This is the type of praise we offer to God in the midst of turmoil or the presence of a challenge. It is sacrificial because someone who hasn't first offered their heart to God will not usually praise and worship Him in the face of difficulties.

When we are good to others and share what we have with them, we offer a sacrifice to God. Hebrews 13: 16 says, ""*And do not forget to do good and to share with others, for with such sacrifices God is pleased*" (NIV). We can stretch out our hands to others through our presence when they need someone to comfort them, or our finances, our love, our kindness, a word of hope or encouragement. We can also share Jesus with those who do not know Him. By making ourselves available in this manner, based on our ability and willingness, we become a channel through which God reaches out to others. One cannot be a channel without a connection to the source, God.

Another avenue of sacrifice is fasting. Fasting is abstaining from the desires of the flesh so that we can focus on God. As we stay away from what the flesh needs, our bodies become weak, and our spirit, comes alive. The strength of our spirit thus enables us to function for the duration of the fast. When our spirit gains strength over our bodies, we find ourselves more in tune with God, for we are spirit beings like Him. Fasting humbles us, as we recognize the power of God to carry us through our seasons of weakness. It builds our reliance on Him. Fasting is a spiritual tool that when combined with prayer, draws us closer to God. Without prayer, fasting is merely a weight loss strategy.

The act of fasting was relevant in the Old Testament and also in the New Testament. In the Bible, fasting is going without food for a while. Moses fasted for forty days, and so did Jesus. Esther did the same for three days. Daniel and his friends stayed away from meat for ten days, having only vegetables and water. Contrary to the belief that fasting is irrelevant today, Jesus said we would need it after His departure from Earth.

"Then the disciples of John came to him, saying, 'Why do we and the Pharisees fast, but your disciples do not fast?' And Jesus said to them, 'Can the wedding guests mourn as long as the bridegroom is with them? The days will come when the bridegroom is taken away from them, and then they will fast'" (Matthew 9:14-15 ESV).

People without medical conditions can fast for as long as they desire, taking into account their mental and physical alertness so they know when to stop. Individuals with medical conditions are advised to seek counsel from their healthcare providers before embarking on this spiritual exercise. I have seen people break away temporarily from other time-consuming and energy-sapping worldly pleasures such as social media to connect with God.

Finally, it is important to state that in the Old Testament God met people at the level and state of their giving. When He gave directions to Moses for the acceptable offerings and sacrifices, including the place where they should be, He said to him, *"It shall be a regular burnt offering throughout your generations at the entrance of the tent of meeting before the Lord, where I will meet with you, to speak to you there. There I will meet with the people of Israel, and it shall be sanctified by my glory"* (Exodus 29:42-43 ESV). The tent of meeting was the place where Moses met with God regularly. Here, God spoke to him as one does with a close friend, face to face (Exodus 33:11). It was at its entrance that God instructed Moses to give the burnt offerings.

Jesus paid the offering for our sins, and our acceptance of what He did on the cross of Calvary guarantees us the presence of God's Spirit (Acts 2:38). We accept Him by believing in Him. No longer do we need a tent offering to meet with God, for our bodies are now His tent. We see this in 1 Corinthians 3:16, *"Don't you know that you yourselves are God's temple and that God's Spirit dwells in your midst?"* (NIV). The tent of meeting in the Old Testament

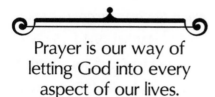

Prayer is our way of letting God into every aspect of our lives.

was set apart and consecrated, because it was God's tabernacle in Israel's midst. Likewise, we are to keep our bodies holy and acceptable, for the Spirit of God now resides in us. The sacrifice we have to pay to keep our bodies sanctified is to cherish it, take care of it, and live a holy life by the power of the Holy Spirit within us. In fact, the presence of God's Spirit in our lives empowers us to make this sacrifice. The more we honour God with our bodies as His tent, the more we pull closer to His presence within and around us. *"Therefore I urge you, brothers and sisters, by the mercies of God, to present your bodies [dedicating all of yourselves, set apart] as a living sacrifice, holy and well-pleasing to God, which is your rational (logical, intelligent) act of worship"* (Romans 12:1 AMP).

Prayer

Prayer is not a one-way conversation with God, where we tell Him what we want, how we want it, and when we want it. *"Pray without ceasing"* (1 Thessalonians 5:17 ESV). Instead, prayer is a two-way conversation, where we speak, and God speaks back to us. Sometimes, the manifestation of what we pray for may not be immediate, so we have no choice but to trust in His Sovereignty.

Luke 5:16 tells us that *"Jesus often withdrew to lonely places and prayed"* (NIV). We need to set aside moments in our day to spend time with God. Most people do this in the morning once they get out of bed. Some prefer the evening before they fall asleep. In my opinion, I do not think God cares that much about the time of the day, as long as we make room for Him daily. However, our morning prayer offers us the opportunity to place our day in His hands before we get started. After the time we have designated to commune with God, our prayer time should not end there. "Praying always" means that we use every opportunity we get to connect with God. It could be as simple as "Lord, thank you for being here with me," when at a traffic stop. Or "God, please show me what to do," when faced with a difficult situation at work. Or "Holy Spirit, please guide my heart as I think, and my lips as I speak at this board meeting." Or "Father, protect my spouse, parents, and children wherever they are at this moment, in Jesus' name."

If Jesus, God in the flesh, separated Himself regularly to pray, then it is a sure sign that we cannot have and maintain a relationship with God without prayer. Any relationship, no matter how intimate, will eventually die if not watered by interaction. Our need to speak often with the significant people in our lives proves to them that they have a special place in our hearts. When we pray regularly, we let God know that we are thinking of Him as much as He is of us. Many people do not enjoy praying, because they do not know what to say. In a healthy relationship, you can speak to a friend, spouse, or child without fear of being reprimanded for what you said or how you said it. See God as that friend, spouse, or child you enjoy open conversations with. Talk to Him about everything. Tell Him about the great things going on in your life. Thank Him for them. Speak to Him about the challenges you are having. Ask for His help in navigating through them. Invite Him to your decision-making and problem-solving table.

Tell Him you are grateful for the people in your life. Talk to Him about the man or woman you met recently and already see the possibility of a future with. Ask Him if He sees the same. In times of confusion, pain, anger, ask Him to reveal His thoughts about the situation to you. Did you contribute to its existence by your actions or inactions? Allow Him to tell you and show you the solution. When at a crossroads, seek His directions and guidance.

Prayer is our way of letting God into every aspect of our lives. Through this medium, we seek His intervention, express our gratitude, know His specific will for us, and inform Him of the happenings in our lives. I've heard people say that God knows about their problem, because He is omnipresent (everywhere), omniscient (all-knowing), and omnipotent (can do all things), so they need not tell Him. While that is true in itself, God does not enter places or circumstances without our invitation. Many testimonies recorded in the Bible happened because people opened the door for Him through their prayer, praise, or some other avenue. It shows our dependence on Him and trust in His infinite ability.

In Matthew 14, Peter walked on water towards Jesus, and at some point he began to sink because of his doubts. Peter cried out, "Lord, save me," and Jesus came to his rescue. Blind Bartimaeus, as we still refer to him even after he received his healing from Jesus, did not get this testimony because he waited for it. He shouted to get Jesus' attention, who at that time was going past him. Jesus stopped and said to him, *"What do you want me to do for you?"* (Mark 10:51). I believe Jesus saw that he was blind before throwing this question at him, the same way He was aware of Peter's sinking. Their invitation to Jesus provoked His actions. The Bible says that we receive from God only when we **ASK**.

Likewise, God expects us to **ASK (Ask, Seek and Knock)** through prayer.

A - Ask. James 4:2c-3 says, *"You do not have because you do not ask. You ask and do not receive, because you ask wrongly, to spend it on your passions"* (ESV).

God desires to be intimate with us. Our inclination to be close to Him is not selfish. Through prayer, we can develop a relationship with Him and also have our needs met, as long as we intend to better our lives with His provision, improve the lives of those around us, and promote His Kingdom with the blessings. He does not expect us to live in stagnation, nor is He pleased when we are only self-centered. Here are some Scriptures that reveals how much God wants us to ask Him for our desires:

"Ask, and it will be given to you" (Matthew 7:7a ESV).

"For everyone who asks receives" (Matthew 7:8a ESV).

"If you, then, being evil [that is, sinful by nature], know how to give good gifts to your children, how much more will your heavenly Father give the Holy Spirit to those who ask and continue to ask Him" (Luke 11:13 AMP).

"Ask of me, and I will make the nations your heritage, and the ends of the earth your possession" (Psalm 2:8 ESV).

"Call to me and I will answer you, and will tell you great and hidden things that you have not known" (Jeremiah 33:3 ESV).

S - Seek. Matthew 7:7b says, *"Seek, and you will find"* (ESV). This promises us that we will find God if we spend time searching. Are you actually seeking in your heart to know God? Are you spending time looking for His presence in your day-to-day activities? There is a story in Luke 15 about a woman who lost one of her ten coins. To find that coin, she became purposeful and took action. She turned on the lights and looked everywhere in her house for it. Seeking is a step higher than asking. We could ask God to reveal Himself to us, but are we taking steps towards finding Him? Remember, the Holy Spirit is always with us. We search because we know He is there. We just need to find Him. Are we taking deliberate steps—praying, reading the Bible and Christian books, meditating, and praising Him—to be more conscious of His presence? Here are some Scriptures about people who did not only ask God, but sought Him desperately:

"Now the Spirit of God came on Azariah the son of Oded, and he went out to meet Asa and said to him, 'Hear me, Asa, and all Judah and Benjamin: the Lord is with you while you are with Him. If you seek Him [inquiring for and of Him, as your soul's first necessity], He will let you find Him; but if you abandon (turn away from) Him, He will abandon (turn away from) you." Now for a long time Israel was without the true God and without a teaching priest, and without [God's] law. But when they were in their trouble and distress they turned to the Lord God of Israel, and [in desperation earnestly] sought Him, and He let them find Him" (2 Chronicles 15:1-4 AMP).

"I will stand and watch and station myself on the ramparts; I will look to see what he will say to me, and what answer I am to give to this complaint" (Habakkuk 2:1 NIV).

"And the one who seeks finds" (Matthew 7:8b ESV).

K - Knock. Knocking is persistence. It takes desire, time, and effort to build genuine relationships. They are not instantaneous. Perhaps you have done all you can to cultivate and improve your relationship with God, and yet He still feels far away. Keep at it. Do not give up, even on your inquiries and petitions. Matthew 7:7c says that we should *"knock, and it will be opened to you"* (ESV). This tells us that unrelenting acts will eventually swing the door open.

In Luke 11, Jesus tells the disciples a story that illustrates what it means to knock tirelessly. A man had unexpected guests show up at his home at midnight. When he realized he had no food for these guests, he went to his friend's house in search of food. But it was past midnight. After spending time knocking on his friends door, the friend answered the door and responded to his buddy's request, not based on their association with each other, but based on his friend's dogged determination not to leave without his desire being granted. Interestingly, in Luke's account, it was after this story that Jesus instructed the disciples to ask, seek, and knock.

Prayer is God's blank cheque to us, and as we **ASK**, filling the cheque lines with our inquiries, petitions, gratitude, and more, we draw closer to the only One who has the power to honour our request. Here are some Scriptural references on knocking:

"But [meanwhile] Peter continued knocking; and when they opened the door and saw him, they were completely amazed" (Acts 12:16 AMP).

"I will wait all the days of my struggle until my change and release will come" (Job 14:14b AMP).

"And to the one who knocks, it will be opened" (Matthew 7:8c ESV).

Think of these strategies of coming nearer to God as making an omelette. We need more than an egg to make this happen; no ingredient is stand alone. For example, we do not just pray and ignore others such as praise or offerings, but incorporate them all in our journey in building a relationship with God.

Chapter Nine

A NEW BEGINNING

"And no one puts new wine into old wineskins. If he does, the new wine will burst the skins and it will be spilled, and the skins will be destroyed. But new wine must be put into fresh wineskins" (Luke 5:37-38 ESV).

THE BIBLE IS full of many interesting, plot twisting, and sometimes hard-to-believe real life experiences that happened before and after the coming of Jesus Christ. One of my favourite stories is Israel's exodus from Egypt after many years of slavery. Many of us are familiar with the ten plagues God inflicted on the Egyptians so that Pharaoh would let the Israelites go. It is mind-boggling to see the extent God will go to in order to bring His children out from troubling circumstances. Moses was chosen to lead the way from their place of agony, Egypt, to their land of glory, Canaan. Moses was a man born to one of the Israelites at a time when Pharaoh, the Egyptian king, had ordered the death of every male child born to an Israelite by throwing them into the River Nile.

Courageously, Moses' mother hid him for three months post-birth. Taking a step of faith, she put him in a basket, layered to impermeability, and placed the basket among the reeds by the bank of the River Nile. Reeds are unstable and effortlessly tossed to and fro by external forces or situations. Her faith was not in the reeds to hold the basket in place, for they lacked the power to do so. Neither was her confidence in herself, for she had done all she could. But the moment she let go of her precious son, God took over. Instead of the River Nile becoming his deathbed, as previously decreed by Pharaoh, it became memorable as the place this tiny patter of feet took his first step into destiny. Interestingly, Pharaoh's daughter came to take her bath in the River Nile, a location designated by her father for the death of innocent babies. What an irony. God has a way of using our enemy to carry out His plans for us. Her eyes caught sight of the basket among the reeds, and upon seeing baby Moses, she decided to adopt him.

Moses grew up in the palace as a prince, educated in the ways of the Egyptians. When the time was right, God began to plant His plan and purpose for him in his heart. The life of Moses was about to flip to the next page of his destiny.

———————◉———————

"So Moses was educated in all the wisdom and culture of the Egyptians, and he was a man of power in words and deeds. But when he reached the age of forty, it came into his heart to visit his brothers, the sons of Israel" (Acts 7:22-23 AMP).

When Moses grew up, He went to visit his brothers as God had impressed on his heart to do. Perhaps God wanted Moses to see firsthand the sufferings of His people, the Israelites, to understand their lived experiences and interact with them, learning more about what it means to be in their shoes, before advocating for them. Sadly, the opposite happened as Moses, who could not stand the injustice done to one of the Israelites by an Egyptian, went ahead and killed the Egyptian. News spread, and in twenty-four hours Moses had become a threat to the very people he tried to save, and an enemy to the people that raised him. He went from being a prince in one of the most powerful nations on Earth at that time to a self-exile.

Moses learned a valuable lesson that should inform many of us. A new beginning is not a new or "wowing" experience that knocks us off our feet. It is not instantaneous. It is not a place where we finally find all the happiness that's bypassed us over the years. A new beginning is a new me and a new you. We must first become new to receive the new. The Scripture tells us in Luke 5:37-38 that putting new wine into old wineskin will lead to the destruction of both the wine and the wineskin. We preserve new wine by putting it into new or fresh wineskin. It would be disastrous for God to take someone from point A to point B without preparing them for the responsibilities that come with being in point B. A new start is a process, not a destination.

> A new beginning is a new me and a new you. We must first become new to receive the new.

A new beginning starts from the journey of transitioning into who God wants us to be in order to possess what He has in store for us. We first become new (fresh wineskin) to receive the blessings God has for us (the wine). On this new path, we will encounter barriers, but God's desire is for a new me and a new you to face those obstacles. It is for a "wiser Moses" to handle conflicts better and make informed decisions in the face of challenging situations. A new you and me will see providence where we'd usually see problems, recognize opportunities in opposition, see the success in failure, and tackle challenges as stepping stones rather than setbacks.

For Moses, the new beginning did not start in the palace, though it was a notable step in his destiny to keep him protected. His fresh start began in the desert, where he ran to for safety. A desert experience is usually the first step in a new season, for it is in this place that the old gives way to the new, if we allow it. Pruning and preparation begin. Our minds get renewed. Perspectives change. Understanding broadens. Wisdom develops and grows. Skills and talents are enhanced. The transformation we go through challenges our worldview, attitudes, beliefs, and behaviour, and we begin to become that new wineskin that can carry the wine successfully.

Those who refuse to start afresh in the desert experiences of life will never grasp the full beauty of new beginnings, for they will attempt to have revolutionary insights with an old mindset, and achieve new results with conventional methods.

When it was time to embark on the mission of Israel's deliverance, the Moses that led them out differed from the Moses who was self-exiled. The cycle of his new beginning had moved from the refining phase of his character in the desert to that of action. Moses was wiser and more patient than before. He'd shifted from being self-dependent to being God-dependent. If the old Moses had set out on this assignment, he would never have made it far with the Israelites without losing his mind. They were a difficult people to lead. The Israelites expected a situational turn-around without a heart turn-around.

Like an army, Israel marched out of Egypt after God dealt terribly with the Egyptians on their behalf. Israel expected to make one big leap from Egypt—the land of their captivity—to Canaan—their promised land from God. At last, they would have their properties and homes, where they would be leaders instead of followers, and masters rather than slaves. And they were not alone on this journey; God led them in a pillar of cloud by day and a pillar of fire by night, and His servant Moses was in their midst. So, you can imagine how disappointed they must have been when they got hemmed in by the Red Sea that obstructed their progress and the Egyptians who came chasing after them. And this was God's chosen route for them. The Israelites cried out and complained to Moses. Moses deferred back to God, who instructed them to move forward.

> God puts us in situations where we cannot go back to our past and we are then challenged to grow, embrace new experiences, and move forward.

"How, Lord?" the Israelites may have wondered.

Sometimes, God puts us in situations or circumstances where the past is no longer an option for us. We cannot go back to who we used to be and do things like we've always done them. We are, therefore, challenged to grow, learn new skills, and embrace new experiences, regardless of what lies ahead or around us. This particular challenge set the stage for one of the most groundbreaking miracles in the Bible. God parted the Red Sea as Israel went ahead. The pathway for Israel's escape became a burial ground for their past (Egypt).

Three days later, a nation that had witnessed the mighty hand of God in the Red Sea complained when they came across the bitter waters of Marah. Memories of what God had done for them were fast fading. God showed Moses the solution to making the bitter water sweet, and not too long after, God led them to Elim, a place with twelve springs of water and seventy palm trees. Here, they refreshed awhile before continuing on their journey. As they went ahead, they encountered another obstacle and rebelled against God and Moses saying, *"Would that we had died by the hand of the Lord in the land of Egypt, when we sat by the pots of meat and ate bread until we were full; for you have brought us out into this wilderness to kill this entire assembly with hunger"* (Exodus 16:3 AMP).

It was only fifteen days after the Israelites had departed the land of their four-hundred-and thirty-year-old captivity, and they had experienced a tremendous amount of God's love evidenced by His presence and acts of protection and provision towards them. Nevertheless, they were relentless in their whining and, at every bump on the road, desired their past. The same past they had cried about. When the Israelites envisioned a fresh start in their lives, they clearly did not envision this. But the reality is that, with God, the journey to Canaan is as significant as Canaan itself. It is in the process that we are changed into who we need to be to embrace and maximize the blessings in the destination. Becoming is as important as possessing. The Israelites stayed the same with their negative mindsets, worldviews, perspectives, and attitudes, all framed by their oppression in the hands of the Egyptians. Even though God wiped their slate clean by delivering them, their reaction to adversity was the same.

———————◆———————

New beginnings attract a higher level of opposition and trials. A new chapter does not mean challenges are absent. It is what we glean in the early seasons of a new beginning that determines the rest of the journey. God was trying to do within the Israelites in the wilderness what He had done within Moses in the wilderness. This was to create greater dependence on Him, higher levels of faith in Him, increased intimacy with Him, instill the fear of Him, and give them deeper insights. God saw ahead what they did not see, so He kept testing them, and they failed almost every time. When they arrived at the boundary of the land they had looked forward to all those years(Canaan), failure to grasp all that God tried to teach them along the way hindered their possession of it. The Israelites were astonished to find giants in the land that God had set apart for them.

"They reported to Moses and said, 'We went in to the land where you sent us; and it certainly does flow with milk and honey, and this is its fruit. But the people who live in the land are strong, and the cities are fortified (walled) and very large; moreover, we saw there the descendants of Anak [people of great stature and courage]'" (Numbers 13:27-28 AMP).

"But the men who had gone up with him said, 'We are not able to go up against the people [of Canaan], for they are too strong for us.' So they gave the Israelites a bad report about the land which

they had spied out, saying, 'The land through which we went, in spying it out, is a land that devours its inhabitants. And all the people that we saw in it are men of great stature. There we saw the Nephilim (the sons of Anak are part of the Nephilim); and we were like grasshoppers in our own sight, and so we were in their sight'" (Numbers 13:31-33 AMP).

These people had everything they needed to succeed; namely, the presence of God, a dynamic leader in Moses, and a formidable warrior in Joshua. However, they failed critically at developing themselves and learning more about God along the way. Nothing had changed in them since the start of this new phase. Complaining to God about their suffering in Egypt propelled their departure from that land, but a similar approach could not get them into Canaan. In other words, we can complain our way out of a problem but can't complain our way into its solution.

What is our attitude in the wilderness experiences of life? Do we see them as the start of something new? Or as the end of something great? If we see them as the beginning of a new thing, we will learn the lessons, build our spiritual muscles, and keep moving towards victory. If it's the latter, any stumbling block on our path will become a reason to return to our place of captivity.

Do we complain to God every chance we get?

Are we waiting to arrive at our Canaan before praising the Lord?

Are we using this season to water our faith in God in order to grow it, draw near to Him, and change the outlook on our circumstances?

Life's interruptions and challenges come unannounced. When God was teaching Israel's hands to fight as they progressed towards Canaan, it was because He knew the battles they would need to fight to take hold of their promise. Isaiah 43:18-19 tells us to forget what has happened in our past, for God will do a new thing. No new territory comes without its valleys and mountains, hurdles to scale and successes to celebrate, battles to fight and victories to win. Of the entire adult generation of Israel, only two men, Joshua and Caleb, entered the next phase of their new beginning in Canaan, for they looked beyond the miraculous acts of the Red Sea division, manna provision, water from the rock, and more, to the Person behind those acts. Their desire to march on, despite opposition, and drive to inhabit the land of their promise stemmed from their personal knowledge of God. *"But the people that do know their God shall be strong, and do exploits"* (Daniel 11:32b KJV).

> Our transition from one level to the next is dependent on who we know, for every stage is designed to give us a new and deeper revelation of God.

As we progress from one phase to another, God's purpose for us becomes more evident. The darkness and confusion begin to pave the way for light and clarity. The path becomes clearer where shrubs and bushes once covered. For me, the leaves began to blossom, again. God had prepared for me in this place new, rewarding, and purposeful relationships, and at the same time, restored some previous relationships. Explanations were unnecessary. These friends and I just picked up where we left off. God gave me a new meaning for my life and directed me to people who could impart wisdom and knowledge to me. One such person was Monica.

I was going through my itinerary for the upcoming weeks when the Holy Spirit asked me to keep a particular date and time open. God had used this season to give me a vision for my life, and He wanted me to start taking steps. Gripped with fear, I prayed and asked Him for a mentor. I needed someone who had walked this path to hold my hand. Following His direction, I began preparations for promotional materials for this date and time. I had no idea what it was, but I knew it was God's voice, and He wouldn't lead me astray. Days later, I got a call from a man I'd met months earlier. There was an event for Christian leaders, and his organization happened to be one of the sponsors. With permission from his management, he invited me to join them at their table. The notice was short, and he hoped I would be able to attend. But this was no problem, because the date and time turned out to be what I had set aside weeks ago.

Hurriedly, I printed my materials and looked forward to my attendance. Even when I was uncertain about God's intention, I was thrilled at the thought of connecting with these leaders. Once there, my eyes caught sight of a woman seated at a different table. I could feel a pull towards her, so I leaned over to the man who had invited me and asked, "Do you, by any chance, know who that woman is?"

He shook his head in the negative.

In between the photo sessions and exchange of pleasantries at the end of the conference, I lost sight of her. After several attempts to find her, I discontinued my search and focused on distributing my pamphlets to those around me. Again, I looked around the hall and convinced myself that she was gone.

"Can I see the brochure in your hands?" I heard someone behind me ask. And there she stood. Her name was Monica.

Though her story is entirely different from mine, we've had similar experiences that influenced our passion. The areas I needed mentoring were her core strengths. Prayerfully considering our meeting, Monica took me under her spiritual wings and provided me godly encouragement and counsel. This entire journey was a gray area when I started out, but every step of obedience I took towards God's leading threw more light on my path and brought new people my way. God tests our obedience to Him to see if we trust Him. If we do not move in line with His direction, we will never see the next step.

I remember one of the early instructions God gave me. He would lay people and situations on my heart and ask me to pray for them in my house. Some of these people would later call me and share their testimonies, even when they never informed me of the problem prior to its solution. But the Holy Spirit did and wanted me to intercede for them. I was obedient, even when it was not convenient.

Then one Saturday evening, just before I went to bed, the Holy Spirit said to me, "*Osayi, when you get to church tomorrow, someone will walk up to you and ask you to join the newly formed intercessory department. That is where you should serve in the church. Say yes.*"

It happened the next day, just as He told me. It was not just my willingness but my obedience in the secret place that led me here.

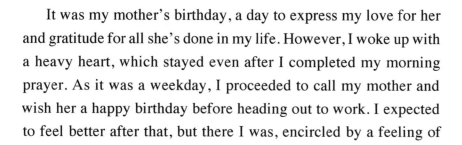

It was challenging at first, being in a new environment and attempting to bring forth a vision. As time went on, I learned to balance the different aspects of my life. Big thanks to my parents and Monica, who reminded me constantly of how important it was for me to fully live while keeping my eyes and mind on the things I was passionate about.

Life was great. I had a supportive family, great friends, a church family whose presence in my life was not restricted to the four walls of the church, a job where working was not a struggle but a daily delight, and a baby in my arms—a vision to nurture. I began writing this book to help others who find themselves lost in the wilderness and who feel forsaken by God to look out for His presence in these situations.

On the road I now travelled on, I never expected to hit a significant bump, powerful enough to throw me off the road and keep me on the curb forever. But this time around, I was stronger and more determined to keep going in the cycle of my new beginning, come what may.

It was my mother's birthday, a day to express my love for her and gratitude for all she's done in my life. However, I woke up with a heavy heart, which stayed even after I completed my morning prayer. As it was a weekday, I proceeded to call my mother and wish her a happy birthday before heading out to work. I expected to feel better after that, but there I was, encircled by a feeling of sadness. Something was not right. By the end of my day, my spirit was more troubled than before. I drove to church that evening to attend a weekday service with the hopes that the sermon and the prayers would uplift my spirit. For a short while, I felt better, until I was ready to go to bed.

Unable to fight off this feeling, I said with a loud voice, "God, please, what is going on?"

Immediately, I heard Him whisper, "*Your daddy.*"

It was night time in Canada and early hours in Nigeria, where he resided at that point. With the seven-hour time difference, my dad and I got accustomed to speaking on the weekends. We'd text each other on weekdays and save our lengthy conversations for the end of the week. I looked forward to talking with him the next day, which was a Saturday. I attributed my emotions to the fact that I missed him. But I did not want to call my dad for fear that he'd pick up the vibes of my sad mood over the phone, and worse, I'd have no explanation for it.

"I'll call him tomorrow," I thought to myself before falling asleep.

At 3:00 a.m., I woke up feeling worse than the previous day. Not knowing what to do anymore, I began singing praises to keep my spirit alive. About an hour later, my phone rang. It was a call from my sister. One I never imagined I'd receive, at least not for the next twenty years.

"Osayi," she said while sniffling. I could tell she was crying, so I sat up, as my heart wondered why. Then I heard my mother weeping in the background, and I knew it was not good.

"Daddy is dead," she finally braced herself to say to me.

"What! Are you sure? Where did you hear this? How did that happen?" I asked in utter disbelief, as I knew he had been well lately.

"His friend called minutes ago from Nigeria. Here's the friend's number," she added as she tearfully gave it to me.

"It happened so quickly, Osayi," my dad's friend said to me when I called him. He sounded so confused and lost. "Your dad and I were traveling to another city when he had a heart attack minutes after we left his house. I was able to get him to the hospital, but sadly, your father just passed away. I am still here with him in the hospital."

I sat still, attempting to digest all I'd just heard. It was only 4:00 a.m. on Saturday morning. I was so stunned and in shock that I could not cry. The confirmation of his death silenced my heart and my mind.

"I'm supposed to speak with him today," I kept saying to myself.

When it hit me that I would never hear his voice again, I burst into tears. My voice of encouragement and support was gone. I no longer had access to that listening ear that paid attention to everything I said, whether it made sense or not. How could God let this happen to me? Where was He when my dad gasped for breath and his heart fought to live? I had questions. All of a sudden, God seemed distant. My dad was my greatest cheerleader, and whenever I pictured milestones in my life, I always saw him next to me. Suddenly, all those images of him by my side were just going to remain mental pictures, and not realities. I was in pain.

I picked up the phone at 5:00 a.m. and called two friends. One of them came within the next hour, and the other showed up a few hours later. Before their arrival, I found myself vacillating between grief and guilt.

"Did God want me to intercede for him at that very hour when He brought him to my mind? Or was He alerting me to my father's exit?"

The more I wavered between these two questions, the more inconsolable I became. I thought about my mother, and my heart bled for her.

When my friend arrived, she tried to find the right words to say. Having commiserated with those whose loved ones had departed this world, I thought there was always a "right" word. However, as I sat that morning on the receiving end of the consolation, there were not enough words she could utter to comfort me. Her warm embrace soothed my aching heart but could not squeeze out the pain, guilt, and disappointment I had inside. Finally, she looked at me and said, "Let us sing praises and worship God. This heaviness that surrounds you needs to leave."

Let me state here that it is not wrong to grieve the loss of a loved one. Grief is normal. But when hopelessness creeps in, it reduces the chance of bouncing back strongly. It traps us in the pit, dimming the outlook, so we do not see beyond the grief. When we allow the truth of God's goodness to find expression in our hearts, it gives us hope. For anyone reading this that may have lost someone dear to them, please know that God is good, even though the situation itself is not. Tell Him how you genuinely feel. Be open and honest with Him. Do you feel pain? Are you angry? Confused? Disappointed? He is the Father and a friend that cares. It may be hard to open up if we think God is behind our sorrow. James 1:17 tells us that every good gift comes from above. Death is not good, but God can bring good out of the pain we feel, if we let Him. Our circumstances and pain are not reflective of His character and ability. He is good all the time. As we dwell on this fact, His comfort and peace will flood our hearts, healing our pain and giving us the courage to trust God, again. There is no reason in life bad enough to make us lose hope, for hope is what fans the flames of life in us, strengthening us in spite of obstacles and causing us to look ahead and go on.

In the Bible, only hope could have triggered Habakkuk's response to an otherwise devastating situation. He said, *"Though the fig tree does not blossom and there is no fruit on the vines, though the yield of the olive fails and the fields produce no food, though the flock is cut off from the fold and there are no cattle in the stalls, yet I will [choose to] rejoice in the Lord; I will [choose to] shout in exultation in the [victorious] God of my salvation"* (Habakkuk 3:17-18 AMP). God ignites this hope in us by keeping us informed of our "Canaan" at the start of a new beginning, so that when we encounter adversities, oppositions, and failure on the pathway, we do not pull over to the curb and retreat into our shell.

Although I did not feel like it, I sang along with my friend. On the surface level, it might have appeared absurd and foolish. Nevertheless, the praise ushered peace and stillness on the inside. The external circumstances did not change; I changed. I still felt pain, but it no longer had the power to consume me. It dawned on me that no matter how bad a situation is, if we look for a reason to praise God, we will always find one. For me, it was the fact that he did not die alone. That was enough for me. We do not arrive in this world alone. At the least, we are guaranteed the presence of our mother. But to depart alone is one of the saddest things to ever happen to anyone. His friend being there at his final moment was simply God giving my dad help when he needed it the most.

My questions remained unanswered, mainly because I felt guilty that I should have prayed that very night God had laid him on my heart. I prayed for my family during my daily devotional time. I came to the realization, through searching the Scriptures and receiving counsel from loved ones, that my actions or inactions could not limit or define God and His abilities. I did not need to allow the devil to deceive me into guilt. Humans are a significant part of God's plan, but in their absence, God will still accomplish His purpose. There are some things I will never understand on this side of eternity, so I accepted that God let me in on what He wanted me to know.

"The secret things belong to the LORD our God, but the things that are revealed belong to us and to our children forever, that we may do all the words of this law" (Deuteronomy 29:29 ESV).

In unloving conditions, God is still love. Nothing will ever change that. I determined that moment that rather than allow my dad's death to deter or paralyze me, I would allow it to propel me into action to do the things I promised him I would, to love others the way he loved me, and to live the life of selflessness I saw him live. I looked out for God and found Him in the serenity that over-shadowed me. It is only God's presence that makes us feel at ease while in the storm. That peace gave me strength to find out from the pages of the Bible what happens to a Christian who transitions to eternal glory. I found God in the wise decisions I made in this unforeseen event. Only He could have guided me outside the power of my emotions. Most importantly, I saw God in the people that surrounded me at this time. The people around us at our weakest moments determine, to a large extent, if we will ever get up and continue moving towards the zenith of our new beginning; or if we will become frozen and remain fixated on the same spot; or worse, retreat and go back to our past.

The power of relationships is reflected in the Biblical story of Moses. As Israel marched forward towards Canaan, they met the Amalekites on the way. Without any provocation from Israel, the Amalekites came armed for war; an unanticipated opposition. Joshua, by the instruction of Moses, led the army of Israel to fight against them. They had to go through this situation in order to proceed on their journey. There were no shortcuts or ways around it. As this went on, something interesting happened. The Bible says in Exodus 17 that as long as Moses had his hands up, a sign of surrender to God and victory in the physical, Israel defeated the Amalekites. Whenever his hands dropped, the Amalekites took the lead. He later got tired, as we sometimes get when overwhelmed by the punches life throws at us. Exodus 17:12 records that Aaron and Hur sat Moses on a stone and held up his hands. By their intervention, Israel had the victory. This fight, though intense, was not even to lay hold of their promised land, but to continue moving in its direction.

My friends held my hands so high emotionally and spiritually that I was able to be a source of encouragement and strength to my mother and siblings. God was in every act of their kindness, their prayers, their presence, their words of encouragement, and their financial support.

God knows the exact training ground for every child of His, and the obstacles on our paths differ. That does not imply that one's journey is more relevant than the other. God sees ahead and prepares us in conformity to His overall design. Every hurdle is a training ground to equip us to handle what lies ahead. What is most important is the wisdom we glean as we travel on this path, the increased strength of character we display in adversity, and the God we get to know for ourselves. Our collective knowledge of God, that is the knowledge of God we have from the minds and experiences of others, can only take us a certain distance. It is our personal knowledge of God that takes us the full length into His plans and leads us to the pinnacle of our new beginnings.

As I move ahead with His plan for me and towards His promise to me, I will never let troubles lie to me that I am alone or that God is not

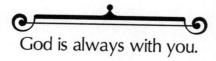

God is always with you.

good, simply because my situation isn't. It does not matter what trials come my way, I'll never have to go through them by myself, for God's promise of His presence is more about His faithfulness than my circumstances.

I encourage you as well, as you go forward in your new season never to allow challenges make your cravings for "Egypt," your past, more desirable than your longing for "Canaan," your future. See new beginnings as a process, and know that every step matters and every experience counts. Scale over the hurdles on your path. Overcome the obstacles that try to stop you. Remain unshakable in the awareness and knowledge that you have company, for God is always with you.

If you will like to have a new beginning and a personal relationship with God, please say this prayer:

Heavenly Father, I thank you for sending Jesus Christ to pay the price for every sinner, and restore them to you. I believe I am a sinner. Today, I accept Jesus Christ as my Lord and Saviour. I know that through His sacrifice, I am cleansed, and made right with you.

Empower me by your Spirit to live a life that pleases you. Make my life count in your Kingdom on earth, and at the end of my earthly life, may I spend eternity with you. Thank you for answering my prayers. I look forward to a new life in Christ. In Jesus name, Amen.

When tempted to think no one cares for you or understands your pain, may these scriptures remind you of God's closeness to you at all times through the Holy Spirit. Meditate on them and allow their truth to sink into your heart.

The following verses are taken from the NIV, unless otherwise stated.

"Then they will know that I, the Lord their God, am with them and that they, the Israelites, are my people, declares the Sovereign Lord." (Ezekiel 34: 30) *"A time is coming and in fact has come when you will be scattered, each to your own home. You will leave me all alone. Yet I am not alone, for my Father is with me."* (John 16:32)

"The Lord replied, 'My Presence will go with you, and I will give you rest.'" (Exodus 33:14)

"I will put my dwelling place among you, and I will not abhor you. I will walk among you and be your God, and you will be my people." (Leviticus 26:11-12)

"'Do not be afraid of them, for I am with you and will rescue you," declares the Lord."* (Jeremiah 1:8)

"All this took place to fulfill what the Lord had said through the prophet: 'The virgin will conceive and give birth to a son, and they will call him Immanuel' (which means "God with us")." (Matthew 1:22-23)

"'They will fight against you but will not overcome you, for I am with you and will rescue you,' declares the Lord." (Jeremiah 1:19)

"'Then you will call on me and come and pray to me, and I will listen to you. You will seek me and find me when you seek me with all your heart. I will be found by you,' declares the Lord, 'and will bring you back from captivity. I will gather you from all the nations and places where I have banished you,' declares the Lord, 'and will bring you back to the place from which I carried you into exile.'" (Jeremiah 29:12-14)

"The Lord your God is with you, the Mighty Warrior who saves. He will take great delight in you; in his love he will no longer rebuke you, but will rejoice over you with singing." (Zephaniah 3:17)

"But Stephen, full of the Holy Spirit, looked up to heaven and saw the glory of God, and Jesus standing at the right hand of God." (Acts 7:55)

"Be strong and courageous. Do not be afraid or terrified because of them, for the Lord your God goes with you; he will never leave you nor forsake you." (Deuteronomy 31:6)

"So do not fear, for I am with you; do not be dismayed, for I am your God. I will strengthen you and help you; I will uphold you with my righteous right hand." (Isaiah 41:10)

"Because God has said, "Never will I leave you; never will I forsake you." (Hebrews 13:5b)

"Do not be afraid, you worm Jacob, little Israel, do not fear, for I myself will help you," declares the Lord, your Redeemer, the Holy One of Israel." (Isaiah 41:14)

"The poor and needy search for water, but there is none; their tongues are parched with thirst. But I the Lord will answer them; I, the God of Israel, will not forsake them." (Isaiah 41:17)

"But now, this is what the Lord says—he who created you, Jacob, he who formed you, Israel: 'Do not fear, for I have redeemed you; I have summoned you by name; you are mine. When you pass through the waters, I will be with you; and when you pass through the rivers, they will not sweep over you. When you walk through the fire, you will not be burned; the flames will not set you ablaze.'" (Isaiah 43:1-2)

"Do not be afraid, for I am with you; I will bring your children from the east and gather you from the west." (Isaiah 43:5)

"Even though I walk through the darkest valley, I will fear no evil, for you are with me; your rod and your staff, they comfort me." (Psalm 23:4)

"In a desert land he found him, in a barren and howling waste. He shielded him and cared for him; he guarded him as the apple of his eye, like an eagle that stirs up its nest and hovers over its young, that spreads its wings to catch them and carries them aloft. The Lord alone led him; no foreign god was with him." (Deuteronomy 32:10-12)

"I will instruct you and teach you in the way you should go; I will counsel you with my loving eye on you." (Psalm 32:8)

"Where can I go from your Spirit? Where can I flee from your presence? If I go up to the heavens, you are there; if I make my bed in the depths, you are there. If I rise on the wings of the dawn, if I settle on the far side of the sea, even there your hand will guide me, your right hand will hold me fast. If I say, "Surely the darkness will hide me and the light become night around me," even the darkness will not be dark to you; the night will shine like the day, for darkness is as light to you." (Psalm 139:7-12)

"I am with you and will watch over you wherever you go, and I will bring you back to this land. I will not leave you until I have done what I have promised you." (Genesis 28:15)

"I will lead the blind by ways they have not known, along unfamiliar paths I will guide them; I will turn the darkness into light before them, and make the rough places smooth. These are the things I will do; I will not forsake them." (Isaiah 42:16)

"I will praise the Lord, who counsels me; even at night my heart instructs me. I keep my eyes always on the Lord. With him at my right hand, I will not be shaken." (Psalm 16:7-8)

"You make known to me the path of life; you will fill me with joy in your presence, with eternal pleasures at your right hand." (Psalm 16:11)

"And surely I am with you always, to the very end of the age." (Matthew 28:20b)

"In the beginning was the Word, and the Word was with God, and the Word was God." (John 1:1)

"Then have them make a sanctuary for me, and I will dwell among them." (Exodus 25:8)

"Do not cast me from your presence or take your Holy Spirit from me. Restore to me the joy of your salvation and grant me a willing spirit, to sustain me." (Psalm 51:11-12)

"Worship the Lord with gladness; come before him with joyful songs. Know that the Lord is God. It is he who made us, and we are his; we are his people, the sheep of his pasture." (Psalm 100:2-3)

"For I will pour water on the thirsty land, and streams on the dry ground; I will pour out my Spirit on your offspring, and my blessing on your descendants. They will spring up like grass in a meadow, like poplar trees by flowing streams." (Isaiah 44:3-4)

"Come near me and listen to this: 'From the first announcement I have not spoken in secret; at the time it happens, I am there.' And now the Sovereign Lord has sent me, endowed with his Spirit. This is what the Lord says—your Redeemer, the Holy One of Israel: 'I am the Lord your God, who teaches you what is best for you, who directs you in the way you should go.'" (Isaiah 48:16-17)

"What agreement is there between the temple of God and idols? For we are the temple of the living God. As God has said: 'I will live with them and walk among them, and I will be their God, and they will be my people.'" (2 Corinthians 6:16)

"Tremble, earth, at the presence of the Lord, at the presence of the God of Jacob, who turned the rock into a pool, the hard rock into springs of water." (Psalm 114:7-8)

"Paul and his companions traveled throughout the region of Phrygia and Galatia, having been kept by the Holy Spirit from preaching the word in the province of Asia." (Acts 16:6)

"I will listen to what God the Lord says; he promises peace to his people, his faithful servants —but let them not turn to folly." (Psalm 85:8)

"God is not human, that he should lie, not a human being, that he should change his mind. Does he speak and then not act? Does he promise and not fulfill?" (Numbers 23:19)

"I am the true vine, and my Father is the gardener. He cuts off every branch in me that bears no fruit, while every branch that does bear fruit he prunes so that it will be even more fruitful. You are already clean because of the word I have spoken to you. Remain in me, as I also remain in you. No branch can bear fruit by itself; it must remain in the vine. Neither can you bear fruit unless you remain in me. "I am the vine; you are the branches. If you remain in me and I in you, you will bear much fruit; apart from me you

can do nothing. If you do not remain in me, you are like a branch that is thrown away and withers; such branches are picked up, thrown into the fire and burned. If you remain in me and my words remain in you, ask whatever you wish, and it will be done for you." (John 15:1-7)

"No misfortune is seen in Jacob, no misery observed in Israel. The Lord their God is with them; the shout of the King is among them." (Numbers 23:21)

"For the Lord your God moves about in your camp to protect you and to deliver your enemies to you. Your camp must be holy, so that he will not see among you anything indecent and turn away from you." (Deuteronomy 23:14)

"And I heard a loud voice from the throne saying, 'Look! God's dwelling place is now among the people, and he will dwell with them. They will be his people, and God himself will be with them and be their God.'" (Revelation 21:3)

"But in their distress they turned to the LORD, the God of Israel, and sought him, and he was found by them." (2 Chronicles 15:4)

"The Lord is near to all who call on him, to all who call on him in truth." (Psalm 145:18)

"The Lord is close to the brokenhearted and saves those who are crushed in spirit." (Psalm 34:18)

ENDNOTES

Chapter Six

[1] Merriam Webster's Dictionary. "Testify."
https://www.merriam webster.com/dictionary/testify

Chapter Eight

[2] Webster's Revised Unabridged Dictionary. "Praise."
http://biblehub.com/topical/p/praise.htm

CPSIA information can be obtained
at www.ICGtesting.com
Printed in the USA
LVHW02s2123251217
560730LV00004B/6/P

9 781545 613030